Policy Analysis in Public Policymaking

Policy Analysis in Public Policymaking

Thomas D. Lynch
Syracuse University

Lexington Books
D.C. Heath and Company
Lexington, Massachusetts
Toronto   London

Library of Congress Cataloging in Publication Data

Lynch, Thomas Dexter, 1942-
  Policy analysis in public policymaking.

  Bibliography: p.
  1. Transporation and state—United States. 2. Program budgeting—
United States. 3. Decision-making in public administration—Case studies.
I. Title.
HE206.2.L9   380.5'0973   74-26508 +
ISBN 0-669-97246-0

International Standard Book Number: 0-669-97246-0

Library of Congress Catalog Card Number: 74-26508

Contents

List of Figures

Preface

This book attempts to clarify what can reasonably be expected of policy analysis as it relates to government decision-making. The scope is limited to the public policymaking process in the United States federal government. The attempt to institutionalize policy analysis, called Planning-Programming-Budgeting (PPB), is the focus. The implementation of PPB in the federal government was one of the few attempts in the world to institutionalize policy analysis as part of the public policymaking process.[1]

"Public policymaking" as a daily, inescapable fact of any government is not the subject here. Instead, the book is concerned with certain processes and considerations that precede decision making and shape its character. The emphasis is on the *making* rather than the *policy*.

In preparing this book, a great deal of careful effort went into assembling information from published sources, official government publications, unusual sources such as trade newsletters, internal government letters and memoranda, and interviews. The goal, particularly in Chapters 2 through 5, was to understand fully the facts and circumstances associated with specific policy decisions, especially the role PPB was expected to play in policymaking and the role it actually did play. If written source material was not adequate to explain the circumstances surrounding a policy decision, then interviews were used to supplement the written material.

The facts cited in Chapters 2 through 5 were documented whenever possible by written data, some of which were unpublished, but which can be inspected independently by anyone wishing to do so. Unpublished documentation in the form of internal government papers was used most often in Chapters 3 and 4, because the author was a minor participant in the events cited in those chapters. The author worked three years in the Urban Mass Transportation Administration as a program analyst in the Office of Program Planning. This day-to-day experience was helpful in assembling information and gaining insight into how decisions were being made. In a few instances, the author used himself as a source, but only in unusual circumstances where no other source of information was available.

Interviews were conducted over approximately a six-month period (January to June 1972), and each interview was carefully recorded. Most interviews were conducted during the lunch period or after working hours. During the interviews, the author constantly sought to determine the correct chronology of events discussed in the interview, to cross-check "facts" stated in other interviews or in written material such as newspaper articles, to follow up leads from other sources, and to identify the interviewee's particular biases. Most of the twenty interviews were conducted with U.S. Department of Transportation high-level career civil servants and Coast Guard officers who were intimately involved in the policy matters discussed. Brief notes were often taken during the interview, but not when the note-taking inhibited frank discussion. After each interview was completed, it was recorded in writing as fully as possible. In all cases, the interviewee was told that he was being interviewed because of his intimate knowledge of the events associated with a given policy decision. In most cases, confidentiality was pledged to protect the interviewees, therefore notes citing interviews normally do not identify the interviewees.

Chapters 1 and 2 present background information essential in terms of understanding PPB and policy analysis and the relationship of each to American administrative thinking. Chapters 3, 4, and 5 present specific case examples of how public policymaking actually took place in three different United States Department of Transportation programs. The final chapter discusses the role of policy analysis in public policymaking.

Thomas D. Lynch
December 7, 1974

1 PPB and the Research Question

On August 25, 1965, President Johnson introduced a Planning-Programming-Budgeting System (PPB) into all federal departments and agencies. The officially stated purpose was to create a managerial tool to help political executives better control programs and budgets.[1] Since that time, PPB has spread to state and local governments and even to other nations.[2] Management tools are created and used because they presumably have a positive impact upon accomplishing work. Does PPB have a positive impact—or any impact—upon the policymaking process? What can reasonably be expected of policy analysis as it relates to governmental decision-making?

Broader Significance

Change and the implementation of change are important considerations in an academic discipline that attempts to understand better "who gets what, when, and how"[3] or the "authoritative allocation of values."[4] Political scientists focus their studies primarily upon the government process and the making of critical policy decisions. The deviation from existing policy- or decision-making processes is by definition change, and change of this kind has been the subject of many articles and publications in political science and public administration.

The administrative change called PPB illustrates the attempted use of formal, systematic, and periodic policy analysis as part of the public decision-making process. Those who argued for this change in administrative practices claimed that governmental decisions and resource allocations would be improved if PPB were implemented. PPB existed officially throughout the federal government between 1965 and 1971, and now it can be critically examined in terms of its actual use. Was the procedure really a significant factor in government decision-making? Or are other factors so important as to have made PPB only an exercise that had little effect on critical government decisions?

These questions are important to political science and public administration because they involve the fundamental assumptions of many who advocate reform. Reformers assume that if only there were more planning and rational thinking, governmental decisions would improve. They then focus their efforts on government reorganization and formal approaches to decision-making, such as PPB. But what if this fundamental assumption is false or far too simple? Reformers might then better direct their energies toward education, partisan politics, or even a more relevant kind of reorganization.

Planning-Programming-Budgeting

The introduction of PPB in the federal government was claimed to be a significant change in American public administration.[5] However, it had strong precedent in earlier measures. The 1965 presidential directive that established PPB was preceded by Secretary Robert McNamara's introduction of program budgeting in the Defense Department in 1961.[6] McNamara's idea, in turn, had precedence in the ideas of Arthur Smithies,[7] Jesse Burkhead,[8] David Novick,[9] Werner Z. Hirch,[10] and others.[11] The ideas of these men were anchored in a half century of tradition and evolution.[12] For example, in 1907 a sample "program memorandum" was published by the New York Bureau of Municipal Research.[13]

President Johnson was said to be impressed by the decision-making process developed in Secretary McNamara's Department of Defense. McNamara was oriented toward rigorous and logical decision-making. He hired key people, such as Charles J. Hitch, who were academically trained in analysis and who believed that analysis could be applied to policymaking in the Department of Defense. They gained a reputation for being successful. President Johnson announced that this "better approach to decision-making" should be extended to all of the federal government and he so ordered in 1965. That PPB was implemented at a time when President Johnson was advocating a guns-and-butter (Vietnam and the War on Poverty) budget should not be overlooked. It is sound politics to implement major management improvements when a president is also asking for large budgets. President Johnson's support of program budgeting could have, in part, stemmed from his desire to appear frugal.[14]

PPB was considered a means of linking planning and budgeting. According to a former director of the Bureau of the Budget, it is "a system that starts with planning about objectives, develops programs through analysis on the basis of those objectives, and translates those programs into budgetary requirements."[15] According to a summary from another source, the primary distinctive characteristics of PPB are that it (1) focuses on identifying the fundamental objectives of the government and then relates all activities to them, (2) explicitly identifies future year implications, (3) considers all pertinent costs, and (4) performs systematic analysis of alternatives.[16]

Origins of PPB: Earlier Budget Reforms

PPB had its origins in several important earlier economic and budget reforms. The most important of these were: the Keynesian emphasis, new microeconomics, systems analysis, and the increasing acceptance of planning on a national scale.

In calling attention to the use of fiscal policy to promote full employment,

Keynesian, or macroeconomic, thinking forced a major new use of the budget function as a tool to achieve economic objectives.[17] This development brought large numbers of economists into top- and middle-level positions of influence in central financial management.[18] It also affected the following changes, which foreshadow PPB in many instances:

1. an expanded, multiple-year time horizon instead of the single-year perspective,[19]
2. more sophisticated data on all government expenditures and revenues, including special funds and loans,[20]
3. longer-term projections (both probability statements and goals) relating such data to other economic variables,
4. more accurate allocations of expenditures and revenues to time periods (this requires more use of the accrual methods of business accounting),
5. distinctions between current and "investment-type" outlays,[21] and
6. classification of total government expenditures by large bundles of programs.[22]

PPB was also influenced by the evolution in micro, or welfare, economics. Welfare economists attempted to structure a science of finance predicated on the principle of marginal utility. By appraising the marginal costs and benefits of alternatives, analysts could determine which combination of expenditures afforded maximum utility.[23] Cost-benefit analysis became the significant analytical tool, particularly in large water-resource development projects. This innovation was criticized on the ground that many of the monetary measures used in the formulas were arbitrary, if not completely fictitious, and that other important measures were neglected. The subsequent, more advanced "cost-effectiveness analysis" was broader, in that it took into account nonmonetary information, such as number of lives saved. This expanded definition of "benefit" somewhat mitigated the older criticisms, but the charge remained that the analyses did not try to account for other causative factors. This charge is valid, because the estimates of presumed results must take into account many causative factors external to the program under analysis.[24]

Systems analysis was another significant contributor to the development of PPB. It evolved from World War II operations research that attempted to coordinate optimally manpower, material, and equipment. E.S. Quade defines systems analysis as "any orderly analytical study designed to help a decision maker identify a preferred course of action from among possible alternatives." He goes on to say, "The phrase 'systems analysis' in the defense community refers to formal inquiries intended to advise a decision-maker on the policy choices involved in such matters as weapon development, force posture design, or the determination of strategic objectives." He cites as typical analyses the tackling of such policy questions as:

what might be the possible characteristics of a new strategic bomber and whether one should be developed; whether tactical air wings, carrier task forces, or neither could be substituted for United States ground divisions in Europe; or whether we should modify the test-ban treaty now that the Chinese Communists have nuclear weapons and, if so, how.[25]

These are the kind of policy questions PPB was intended to help answer for government agencies.

PPB required an enormous information handling capacity and a method of analyzing many complex alternative solutions to problems. New technological developments, such as computers, made it possible to cope with the first problem; systems analysis furnished much of the methodology for the analysis of alternatives.

The acceptance of planning in American government, the latest development in the evolution of PPB, is relatively new. The national government has been reluctant to embrace central planning of any sort because central planning was identified by many people with socialist management of the economy. The National Resources Planning Board (1939-43) did serve a national-planning function, but its existence and short duration were largely due to the war. Today, however, the Council of Economic Advisers, the National Security Council, the Domestic Council, the Cabinet Committee on the Environment, and the Council on Rural Affairs all have planning responsibilities.[26] Planning responsibilities, for example, are an integral part of the following specific functions of the Domestic Council:

1. assessing national needs, collecting information and developing forecasts for the purpose of defining national goals and objectives;
2. identifying alternative ways of achieving objectives, and recommending consistent, integrated sets of policy choices;
3. providing rapid response to presidential needs for policy advice on pressing domestic issues;
4. evaluating national priorities for the allocation of available resources; and
5. maintaining a continuous review of on-going programs from a policy standpoint, and proposing reforms as needed.[27]

This shift toward the increased credibility of planning has been rapid. Urban planning, through section 701 grants, has led to extensive local and metropolitan area planning. Currently, planning is required in many federal programs, and state planning agencies are becoming more common. PPB in the over-all federal budgeting process was a logical extension of this trend toward planning.

The two activities of budgeting and planning have begun to merge in spite of their disparate perspectives: the one is conservative and negativistic; the other, innovative and expansionist. The long lead-time in the development and procurement of hardware and capital investments, the diversity of government agencies involving related activities, and the sheer growth of federal programs have made necessary a more rational approach to policy analysis and the allocation of resources. There is a trend toward emphasizing planning and merging it with budgeting, but the planning orientation is not yet dominant, especially in its relationship to current budgeting reality.[28]

PPB: One Use of Analysis

According to William M. Capron, an assistant director of the Bureau of the Budget when PPB was introduced, the proponents of PPB were motivated by a desire to bring more analysis to government decision-making.

I know from my own experience that one of the principal factors which motivated people in the Budget Bureau to insist on a greater use of analysis has been the fact that, typically, both program and budget recommendations coming to the President from the departments and agencies have not contained any alternatives and have denied the President the option of making meaningful choices. The options have been screened out before the President has had an opportunity to choose among them. This great failure is frustrating to the Budget Bureau and to the President. Moreover, not only is the typical budget request as it comes forward to the Budget Bureau lacking in alternatives, but there is not even available to the Budget Director and the President he advises the kind of information which allows one to judge the effect on a given program of either a decrease or an increase in the funding level finally recommended to the Congress. The result of this is that the judgment of Budget Bureau staff is often superimposed on the judgment of those presumably much more knowledgeable about the program and the Budget Bureau inevitably acts, at least sometimes, in a very arbitrary fashion—arbitrary because those required, say, to cut X-hundred million dollars from a given program area have nothing before them to indicate the impact of the cut, or the impact of the manner in which they allocate that cut among various program elements.[29]

As it was conceived, PPB was not analysis, but was a defined use of analysis calling for a program structure, a five-year program and financial plan, a revised extended budget cycle, and a key document called a program memorandum. The actual application of analysis varied greatly from department to department and even from agency to agency within a department. There was, however, a standard form of analysis demanded by the Bureau of the Budget, which became the Office of Management and Budget in 1971. This use of analysis was to be the significant way to decide policy, including resource allocation decision. PPB was not meant to be coextensive with the general concept of analysis; instead, PPB was to be merely one approach to, and use of, analysis in making major policy decisions.

Analysis, on the other hand, is a much broader concept, which can be characterized as "various art forms which go under the generic heading of 'analysis'."[30] Generally speaking, analysis is laying out alternatives for those who must make decisions. It involves assumptions and objectives, defining and testing alternatives, and comparing alternatives with a methodological objective of making recommendations or findings useful in deciding policy questions. Most commentators on analysis would say that it also involves examining costs (and possibly benefits) and comparing the alternative's effect on established objectives. Most would point out that several cycles of analysis may be necessary before the final recommendations are cited with refined objectives, alternatives, and findings.[31]

The forms of analysis, used in connection with and separately from PPB, include cost effectiveness, benefit-cost, sensitivity analysis, break-even analysis, A Fortiori analysis, diminishing marginal utility, pay-off matrix, isoquants, and present values.[32] The key to analysis is its usefulness to the decision-making process. The analyst decides how the alternatives are expressed and the explicit measures used. This makes the analyst an actor in the decision-making process, but analysis itself does not make decisions, except in those areas where assumptions are very clearly established or the decision-maker merely adopts the conclusions of the analyst.[33] The forms of analysis are quite varied, from something as simple as a four-cell pay-off matrix, which lays out effects associated with two different circumstances, to a complex benefit-cost study. The pay-off matrix can help us decide to take rain clothes under a given set of circumstances. A benefit-cost analysis can help us decide to build a multimillion dollar dam because benefits exceed cost for that given project. The form of analysis chosen depends upon the subject being analyzed, but many different forms or techniques are available. PPB was one use of analysis defined for all government departments and agencies. This does not mean that other approaches to analysis could not be used, but that only one approach was mandated as a common denominator or tool for decision-makers.

Decision-Making Models

The following brief introduction to various decision-making models will clarify how public policymaking does occur and the potential role of policy analysis in making policy. The major and commonly noted models are Charles E. Lindblom's incremental change model, Aaron Wildavsky's budgetary process model, Herbert A. Simon and James G. March's satisficing model, the ideal rational model, and Yehezkel Dror's optimum model. To this list, a provocative but little-cited model can be added: Richard Wallen's "stages of problem solving" model.

Charles E. Lindblom's incremental change model is a descriptive one; it points out that policy is made by a "muddling through" process. Major public policies evolve through cautious incremental steps; political forces mutually adjust their positions and, over time, public policy changes. Although it is only descriptive, Lindblom's model is often used for normative purposes to advocate a fundamentally conservative approach to policy innovation because it implies change comes almost entirely through marginal policy shifts.[34] Professor Dror, like many other students of the phenomenon of public policymaking, points out that the Lindblom model is an excellent descriptive aid but biases the analyst against more radical innovative alternatives that do occur and are significant.[35]

A highly significant theoretical model used in political science and public administration is found in Aaron Wildavsky's *The Politics of the Budgetary Process.* The model addresses itself to the very important budgetary process, in the course of which many key policy decisions are made. Wildavsky's thinking is similar to that of Lindblom. An agency develops and advocates a budget to its department, the Office of Management and Budget, and to Congress. In those major phases of the process, the agency takes the role of an advocate, the reviewer (e.g., Office of Management and Budget) questions the wisdom of the proposal, and the reviewer makes a tentative decision, which is often appealed to the secretary, the president, or the Senate. Wildavsky explains these roles very well, but his model is limited to the budgetary process.[36]

Herbert A. Simon and James G. March have created a much more general public policymaking model with their concept of satisficing. When we, as decision-makers, are confronted with the need to make a decision, we start searching for alternatives. As soon as we find one that satisfies our criteria, we look no further. Policymakers identify obvious alternatives based on their recent personal experiences. If they find an alternative that is satisfactory in terms of its pay-off, they choose this alternative without trying to find additional alternatives that would have a higher pay-off. Alternatives are searched for only until one with a satisfactory pay-off is found. The search is curtailed largely because of human inertia and the strength of conservative forces in an organization. In reality, identifying even one satisfactory alternative solution is quite an achievement, considering the difficulties. Policymakers should aim for this goal, according to Simon, rather than the utopian goal of finding the optimal alternative.[37]

The rational model is most commonly cited as the ideal way to reach decisions, especially major public policy decisions. Its assumptions are deeply rooted in modern civilization and culture. According to Dror, the model systematically breaks decision-making down into six phases:

1. establish a complete set of operational goals, with relative weights allocated to the different degrees to which each may be achieved;
2. establish a complete inventory of other values and resources with relative weights;
3. prepare a complete set of the alternative policies open to the policymaker;
4. prepare a complete set of valid predictions of the costs and benefits of each

alternative, including the extent to which each alternative will achieve the various operational goals, consume resources, and realize or impair other values;

5. calculate the net expectation for each alternative by multiplying the probability of each benefit and cost for each alternative by the utility of each, and calculating the net benefit (or cost) in utility units; and

6. compare the net expectations and identify the alternative (or alternatives, if two or more are equally good) with the highest net expectation.[38]

Dror's version of the rational model is imposing. In fewer words, the rational model is merely defining one's goals, analyzing the alternatives available, and selecting the alternative that best meets the goals.

Yehezkel Dror argues that the various models are inadequate and that we should use instead his optimal model. Professor Dror points out that the accounts of actual policymakers point to the use of extrarationality, or intuition, and judgment. Dror cites the "Prisoner's Dilemma" to demonstrate value of non- or extra-rationality decision-making. The story states that two persons commit a robbery and are later arrested. The police have evidence that they stole a car for the robbery, but they have no solid evidence of the men committing the robbery. If both are quiet, each will get a five-year sentence. The states attorney approaches each separately and says that the prisoner who makes a complete confession will be released and the other will be prosecuted on both counts (twenty years). However, if both confess, a legal technicality would force the prosecutor to charge both prisoners with two counts. In this case they would each receive lighter sentences (fifteen years). Using the rational model, both prisoners will talk and receive fifteen years; if they follow a hunch and keep quiet, however, they would each save ten years. In this instance, rationality is inferior to extrarationality.[39] The difficulty is that we all do not have good hunches.

Dror's optimal model, the one he advocates, has both rational and extrarational characteristics, uses extensive feedback, concerns itself with the policy of making policy, and is more qualitative in design than other models. He argues that the extrarational complements the inadequacies of the rational model. He believes that a quest for rationality may be too costly and that this consideration must be weighted heavily. Dror argues that the "policy" for making policy (called the metapolicymaking phase) is very significant, for it allows the policymakers to improve the policymaking process. Feedback provides the "intelligence information" needed to take into account the impact of one's policy so that it can be modified to achieve the desired effects.[40]

Major policy changes have often come about because someone in authority says "This is a problem" and then investigates what can be done to solve the problem. In many cases demands for analysis arise not because someone says a given objective is not being met but rather because someone in authority perceives a problem.[41] The "stages of problem solving" model serves to explain the process of policy analysis as it exists in policymaking.[42]

The "stages of problem solving" model was developed by the late Richard Wallen. As Edgar H. Schein points out, the Wallen model is amenable to observation and analysis.[43] It is a useful theoretical tool for both descriptive and normative purposes, for it can be used to describe and explain the decision-making that occurs as well as to guide persons on how to better arrive at decisions.

In the "stages of problem solving" model, the starting point is the perception that a problem exists. Either formally or informally, the decision-maker defines the problem, considers solutions, and analyzes the alternatives. A key decision is

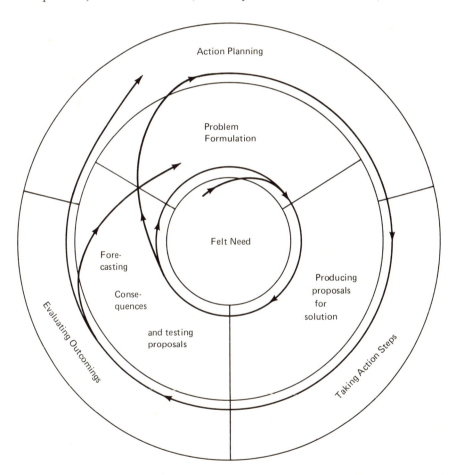

Figure 1-1. Stages of Problem Solving

made either to reconsider the nature of the problem or to plan to resolve the problem. If the decision is to proceed, the necessary action steps are taken and outcomes are evaluated. From evaluation, the decision-maker may either start over by reconsidering the problem or replan his action steps.[44]

Research Questions

Can the implementation of systematic analysis improve governmental policy decisions? William M. Capron asserted at the 1966 American Political Science Association Annual Conference that three claims could be made:

—the *dialogue* between the parties involved (the bureaus, the departments, the Executive Office of the President, the Congress, the private interest groups and "constituencies") will be conducted differently and will certainly be "impacted" by PPB
—*some* decisions will be different from what they otherwise would be without this approach
—and *some* of these decisions will be *better* than they would have been absent the use of more formalized analysis.[45]

This book will not necessarily substantiate these claims; it will merely attempt to shed some additional light on the subject after examining the application of PPB in three Department of Transportation programs. Some have claimed that systematic analysis in government, such as PPB, is doomed to failure, considering the political nature of government policy decisions; the congressional appropriation and budget process, and the human dispositions found in any organization. Is or can policy analysis be a meaningful part of public policymaking? What can reasonably be expected of policy analysis as it relates to public policymaking?

2 PPB in the Department of Transportation

The significant change made by PPB was to lengthen substantially the early part of the budget cycle. The older budget cycle consisted of (1) agencies submitting their requests to the department; (2) the department refining those requests and passing them on to the Office of Management and Budget (OMB), the office responsible for drafting the entire federal budget; (3) OMB drafting the president's budget and the president submitting it to Congress; (4) agencies submitting supporting budget material to appropriation subcommittees; (5) Congress appropriating funds; and (6) OMB then apportioning money to the departments and agencies. With the institution of PPB, agencies were required to perform specific analyses and exercises prior to the first agency budget submission. These analyses were performed according to the guidance of higher-level offices and agencies.

Guidance is the instruction on policy and procedure that higher-level offices and agencies in the executive branch give to lower-level offices and agencies. It is transmitted in printed documents having various titles. The policy and procedural guidance documents of the Office of Management and Budget, for example, are called OMB circulars and bulletins. The departmental guidance documents in the DOT are called orders and notices. The Urban Mass Transportation (UMTA) and the Federal Highway Administration (FHWA) documents are also called orders and notices. The Coast Guard documents are called manuals. The guidance documents from one administrative level are meant to shape administrative practices at all lower levels. For example, the OMB guidance on PPB applied to all federal departments and agencies, and the DOT documents applied to all the subunits in the department. Thus, UMTA and its subunits had to conform to OMB circulars and bulletins, DOT orders and notices, and UMTA orders and notices.

OMB Guidance

The guidance on PPB for the entire federal government was contained in the United States Office of Management and Budget Circular A-11 and Bulletin No. 68-9. These documents show the PPB system to be made up of the following elements: the program memoranda, special analytical studies, program and financial plans, major program issues, and program structure.[1] In general, both departments and agencies were responsible for preparing each PPB element on their own level; departments used the lower-level agency documents as input for compiling their own PPB documents.

In the program memoranda (PM), departments were required to state program objectives and to compare the cost and effectiveness of alternative methods of accomplishing the objectives. Also required were the secretary's recommendations on programs to be carried out, and the reason for those decisions. PMs were meant to be the documentation for the first strategic decisions of the coming budget year.

Special analytic studies (SAS) were analyses of critical problems. They included recommendations on these subjects. Some SASs sought solutions to or better ways of handling specific problems in the budget year; others, such as data-gathering studies, had long-term application. SASs were generally considered to be the most fruitful PPB activity.

The program and finance plan (PFP) was a comprehensive multiyear summary of the department's programs in terms of their output, costs, and financing needs. The planning period extended at least over the budget year plus four future years. The PFP was designed to be the basic planning document of the PPB system.

Departments were also asked to designate major program issues (MPI). These would be policy questions that required a policy determination in the current budget cycle, involved major future-year funding implications, or were fundamental policy choices. A complete MPI included identification of specific alternative courses of action, a discussion of each alternative, and pertinent legislative implications.

The program structure was a logical grouping or typology of departmental activities. The cited criteria for a "good" program structure were that it: (1) facilitated comparison of the cost and effectiveness of alternative approaches to departmental objectives, (2) was objective-oriented, that is, grouped activities with common objectives, and (3) normally involved not more than three levels within a department, that is, the structure outline would not be more detailed than three program subdivisions.

DOT Guidance

PPB existed formally in the DOT from 1968 to 1971, when it was abolished.[2] (It continues to exist informally in many of the activities and sections of the department.) Guidelines for the development and implementation of PPB within DOT were established by DOT Order 2400.2A, dated January 15, 1968.[3] (PPB in DOT was organized late because the department itself was not established until 1967.) On June 29, 1971, the department cancelled the earlier order and issued interim procedures for the FY 1973 program planning and budgeting process. (The changed procedures were necessary not only because the Nixon administration had decided after three and a half years in office to abolish and replace PPB, but also because of a general failure of PPB at the department level.)[4]

Like many departments, the DOT decentralizes much of its decision-making to subdepartment level units called, in most instances, "administrations." Some examples of these units in the DOT are the Urban Mass Transportation Administration, the Federal Highway Administration, the Federal Railroad Administration, and the Federal Aviation Administration. The Coast Guard, although not labeled "administration," also belongs in this category. The department also has "secretarial offices," which are high-level staff units headed by an assistant secretary, such as Office of the Assistant Secretary for Policy and International Affairs. The department itself is headed by a secretary, an undersecretary and a deputy undersecretary. Executive control of DOT is assigned to the undersecretary and the deputy undersecretary. Two important staff units report directly to the undersecretary: the Office of the Budget and the Office of Planning and Program Review. The Office of Planning and Program Review was responsible under PPB for directing and reviewing what were commonly considered the PPB products, i.e., the program proposals and the special analytic studies. The Office of Budget was responsible for preparing the commonly considered budget products of the department. Under PPB, the two offices maintained separate identities, even though theoretically the planning and budgeting processes were merged.[5]

As explained earlier, the innovation of the PPB system was that it required more analytical work prior to the first agency budget submission than did the previous budget system. Thus, each operating administration and secretarial office of DOT was responsible for preparing the analysis and input for PPB. The secretary and others formulated or altered policy, but the administrations and secretarial offices were expected to advance agency and departmental policy positions, which were then subject to revision at the department level. Submissions from the administrations and secretarial offices were called program proposals. These were intended to provide basic program recommendations and justifications to the secretary, including major legislative proposals. Program proposals were meant to be self-contained and include all the information needed to arrive at the recommended policy position. Program data summaries (PDS) were designed to present the details of cost, outputs, and benefits as well as to supplement the program proposals. Other submissions existed for specialized purposes and need not be covered here.[6]

At the department level, the PPB system consisted of "(a) the identification of objectives, (b) the development of a Program Structure, and (c) the production of products in the form of Program Memoranda, Program and Financial Plans, Special Studies, Budget Schedules and related materials."[7]

UMTA Guidance

The UMTA, a part of the DOT, administers several programs dealing with improving intracity transit: (1) a research, development, and demonstration program on urban transportation; (2) a technical studies program that grants money to local governments so that they can study their urban transportation problems and devise the necessary solutions; (3) a capital grant program that grants money to local governments so that they can buy the necessary capital equipment they need in order to save, improve, and extend their transit systems (including, potentially, the building of entirely new rapid-rail transit systems); and (4) a training program that grants money to universities and local governments to upgrade the management training in the transit industry.[8]

UMTA established guidance on PPB with its UMTA Order 2400.1, dated December 12, 1969. PPB in UMTA was meant to be an instrument for executive direction and management.

The UMTA Planning-Programming-Budgeting System is an orderly process for the timely and considered development of a program plan. The plan is the product of a set of structural reports designed to meet the decision-making needs of the Administrator, the Office of the Secretary, and the Executive Office of the President. In addition, it will serve as the basis for the Administrator's management, direction and control of UMTA activities. This includes: identification and selection of objectives (i.e., broad social purposes of the program); establishment of operational goals (specific and measurable impacts to be achieved); identification and evaluation of alternative programs, projects and resource levels; justification and explanation of recommended programs and resource allocations, orderly execution of approved program and project plans, realistic appraisal of progress in program execution; continuing evaluation of the effectiveness of programs and projects; and compliance with requirements for program coordination, accounting, and funds control.[9]

The chief office for PPB in UMTA was the Office of Program Planning, which developed the program proposal; the Office of Administration was responsible for the budget function. Other UMTA offices submitted material to the Office of Program Planning as input for the program proposal and to the Office of Administration in order to support the budget process.

The major components of PPB in UMTA included those already mentioned departmental documents (program proposal and special studies) and documents unique to UMTA: UMTA plan, program change proposal, UMTA studies, progress reports, and program evaluation reports. The UMTA plan was intended to be the key management and program planning document within UMTA. It included, according to the UMTA order,

a detailed *Operating Budget and Financial Plan* for the current fiscal year, providing the basis for execution of short-range plans, compliance with fiscal or program limitations, appraisal of management effectiveness, identification of appropriate corrective action, and evaluation of program effectiveness; (b) the program and budget recommendations pending before Congress (or the results of Congressional action on those requests); (c) the Administrator's decisions and recommendations for the budget year and (d) UMTA's long-range plans for five years beyond the budget year, reflecting the future-year implications of the budget year recommendations.[10]

The other PPB components were supposed to support and complement the UMTA plan. The program change proposal was the formal submission by the other UMTA offices to update the UMTA plan. The UMTA studies were in-depth analyses needed for program recommendations made in the plan. The progress reports were status reports on the programs prepared by the UMTA offices. The program evaluation report was an annual report prepared by the Office of Program Planning, which was intended to give an independent in-depth evaluation of program effectiveness.[11]

Coast Guard Guidance

The Coast Guard is an organization of approximately 60,000 people with district offices and many field units, mostly within the United States. The United States Coast Guard Guidance on PPB, titled *Planning and Programming Manual,* is still being used.[12] The guidance is detailed, sets forth staff responsibilities, procedures, and timetables for action involved in the planning and programming cycles of the Coast Guard. The *Planning and Programming Manual* sets forth the formal policy and budgetary decision-making process.[13]

There are thirty-five essential definitions in the Coast Guard PPB vocabulary cited in the appendix of the manual (Figure 2-1). The PPB system is viewed as three interrelated parts. The "planning" part includes the initial studies and policy determinations. "Programming" is considered to be the detailing of the policy decision, presentations to the department, and submissions requesting authorization legislation. (Legislative authorization is required for most Coast Guard projects costing over $25,000.) "Budgeting" is the development of the submissions to OMB and the congressional appropriation committees, as well as the carrying out of the operating budget.[14]

The lead responsibility for PPB in the Coast Guard is assigned to the chief of staff. The several division heads report to him, among them the Program Division, Plans Evaluation Division, and the Budget Division. The major headquarters office heads also report to the chief of staff. Those offices include the major functional offices, such as Office of Chief Counsel, Office of Operation, and Office of Research and Development. There are also field units: two area offices, twelve district offices, and fifteen "headquarters units."[15]

The process works in three stages. The field units submit their requests to

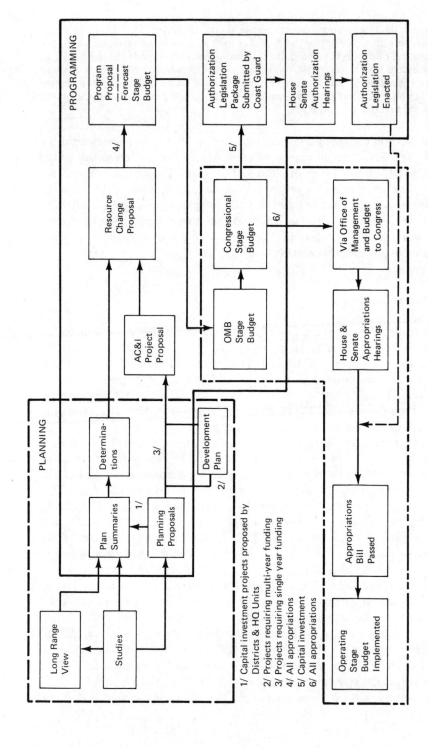

Figure 2-1. Block Diagram for Resource Planning and Program Process. Source: U.S. Coast Guard, *Planning and Programming Manual*—1971, p. III-3.

PROGRAMMING

Program Proposal — Forecast Stage Budget

Authorization Legislation Package Submitted by Coast Guard

House Senate Authorization Hearings

Authorization Legislation Enacted

Resource Change Proposal

4/

5/

Congressional Stage Budget

6/

Via Office of Management and Budget to Congress

AC&I Project Proposal

OMB Stage Budget

House & Senate Appropriations Hearings

PLANNING

Determinations

3/

Development Plan

2/

Plan Summaries

1/

Planning Proposals

Long Range View

Studies

Appropriations Bill Passed

Operating Stage Budget Implemented

1/ Capital investment projects proposed by Districts & HQ Units
2/ Projects requiring multi-year funding
3/ Projects requiring single year funding
4/ All appropriations
5/ Capital investment
6/ All appropriations

"program managers," who generally correspond to office heads under the chief of staff. These groups prepare their documentation and requests and submit them to the appropriate division heads, who report directly to the chief of staff. The division heads then provide the necessary input to follow the PPB system explained above and in Figure 2-1.

The major components of PPB include the already mentioned departmental documents (e.g., program proposals and special studies) but also documents unique to the Coast Guard: planning proposal, plan summary, development plan, determinations, AC and I project proposal reports, and a resource change proposal. Planning proposals are submissions from district or headquarter units which recommend change with respect to existing plans or facilities. They are the first notice of request changes, whereas the development plan is a more detailed explanation of the change. The AC and I project proposal report is an exact report of what the proposed change entails. A plan summary is presented for each individual program and explains the future-year program levels for the near term (one-to-five years), midterm (six-to-ten years), and long term (ten years and beyond). Determinations are analyses of unresolved questions, which are presented to the commandant, and once resolved, these serve as a planning guide for the programs. A resource change proposal is a request for an increase or decrease in a program or a shift in resources from one program to another.[16]

PPB in Reality

Official guidance existed on every level concerning the use of PPB for public policymaking; the objective of this book is to examine actual practice when it came to decision-making in the Department of Transportation. Subsequent chapters detail a few significant program decisions made in the various subunits of DOT during the time PPB was officially in effect. (PPB in DOT began in the last year of the Johnson administration (1969), but the greater part of its existence was during the Nixon administration, with John Volpe as secretary.)

A look at one special analytical study illustrates the use of PPB in the Department of Transportation. A study was conducted by the Federal Aviation Administration on a new radar control system that promised to improve substantially the air traffic controller's capacity to monitor aircraft. The Office of Planning and Program Review would not approve funding of the project, however, on the basis that the results of the study were inadequate to justify going ahead with it. The report was reworked several times to try to make a reasonable case for approving the new system, but still the project was not approved. Ultimately, however, the department decided to fund the project in spite of the lack of adequate rationale.[17]

Another example illustrating the department's use of study results concerns the tentative decision to expand National Airport in Washington, D.C. In this case, all studies recommended that National Airport not be expanded, but the undersecretary made the decision to expand it. Subsequently, the secretary had second thoughts on this subject, and the decision was "tabled." At no time, however, did a PPB analysis influence any decision on this subject.[18]

At the subdepartment level, the use of PPB in actually making policy decisions varied greatly. The Federal Highway Administration (FHWA) ignored PPB as much as possible. FHWA had and has a decision-making process that relies on analysis, but that work had nothing to do with PPB except in unusual situations.[19] In the UMTA, most of the PPB requirements were ignored or never implemented. Two major and significant exceptions did occur. The program proposal was prepared yearly and, at least in some areas, did represent a serious effort to arrive at an agency policy position using analysis. Second, UMTA did prepare a special study analyzing a major policy matter which is still very controversial today and which will be explained in detail in Chapter 4.[20] The next two chapters, in fact, present the details of several of the UMTA policymaking situations and how PPB related to those decisions.

The Coast Guard is one agency where PPB was, and still is, used to make policy decisions. The accomplishment by those in the Coast Guard stands in stark contrast to the other attempts at using PPB in the department. Chapter 5 illustrates how PPB is used in the Coast Guard.

The above brief vignettes of situations in which PPB was overridden or not used provide something of the over-all climate for PPB in DOT. The reasons why PPB as a decision-making system was ignored or overridden in DOT except for the Coast Guard application are discussed in detail in subsequent chapters.

3 Research on Urban Transportation

Research on urban transportation has been an active program since it was authorized in 1964.[1] First carried out in the Urban Transportation Administration of the Department of Housing and Urban Development (HUD), it later became the responsibility of the Urban Mass Transportation Administration (UMTA) in the new Department of Transportation.

Program Overview

Urban transportation research is known as RD&D (research, development, and demonstration) in the UMTA and as R and D in most other agencies. In the first few years, while the initially low budget RD&D program was still in HUD, it was administered by William Hurd, a career civil servant who was the head of the Urban Transportation Administration.[2] Hurd was a strong-willed administrator who ran his programs on consistent principles. In a subsequent position as manager of capital grant and technical studies program in UMTA, he demonstrated his belief that federal assistance funds should be dispersed with the *minimum* amount of "strings" attached by the law. The assistance, he believed, must be administered with an awareness of political realities and the caution necessary to avoid scandal and embarrassing press comments. A minimum of project administration is called for at the federal level, with a maximum amount of trust given the local government sponsor. Hurd operated on the belief that most grantees will desire more money, and that the grantee will not jeopardize this continuing assistance.[3]

Hurd's philosophy is reflected in the way he ran the earliest urban transportation RD&D program.[4] Unlike most R and D activities, the emphasis in his program was on "demonstrating" already accepted innovations in local areas where the innovations were not feasible without federal help because of local fiscal conditions and the conservative attitude of local transit officials. No effort was made to gather information on a systematic control basis. Instead, the money was granted with minimum federal supervision.[5]

When the Urban Transportation Administration was moved over to the new DOT, it became the Urban Mass Transportation Administration and was significantly upgraded in importance, becoming (on paper) a coequal of the Federal Highway Administration (FHWA); the staff was increased from 59 in FY (Fiscal Year) 1969 to 312 by FY 1971.[6] Paul Sitton was appointed the first

UMTA administrator. Administrator Sitton had a very pragmatic approach to government. He believed emphasis in the RD&D program should be placed upon demonstrating the value and advantages of improving mass-transit facilities in cities. He initiated the Central City Project in Seattle, Atlanta, Dallas, Denver, and Pittsburgh. The goals, in each case, were to decide on near-term projects that could be undertaken to improve local transit, to conduct the projects, and to generalize from those efforts the kind of program and policy direction the government should undertake to solve the urban transportation problem. Sitton was administrator in 1968 and 1969, and the Central City Project was just starting to produce some preliminary results when President Nixon appointed Carlos Villarreal as UMTA administrator.[7]

The new administrator came to UMTA with no knowledge of urban transportation or research. He was a former naval officer, engineer, and vice-president of Marquardt, a medium-sized aerospace company. Within a few months, it was obvious that Villarreal wished to disassociate himself from the previous Democratic research policies and wanted to emphasize hardware demonstrations.[8]

One of the new administrator's first acts was to recruit Robert Hemmes as assistant administrator for research. Dr. Hemmes was a Stanford professor of industrial engineering, a close personal friend and former Annapolis classmate of the administrator, as well as a friend of the new undersecretary and others.[9]

Dr. Hemmes, like the new administrator, brought to the program a strong desire to recast it into a "scientific" effort designed to research, develop, and then demonstrate new hardware innovations. He was strongly prejudiced against the Hurd approach of simply assisting urban areas to accept transit innovations that could not be attempted without federal support. He did not concur with the Sitton approach of tailoring demonstrations to the urban political setting and trying to develop insights from that experience. He also questioned the New Systems Study (see following section) because it did not have a rigorous quasi-experimental design associated with the proposed research. Dr. Hemmes believed that the emphasis should be placed upon hardware development and demonstrations, but, significantly, only that kind of hardware development and demonstration that would have a high probability of near-term improvement in existing transit, as opposed to completely new forms of transit.[10]

One interesting series of events illustrates part of Dr. Hemmes's thinking about the direction of the RD&D program. Hemmes inherited a group of projects called service development projects, which were oriented to improving urban mobility for the transportation disadvantaged: the young, old, poor, handicapped, and unemployed. These projects started in the Johnson administration as a reaction to the Watts riot. The first project was a bus "demonstration" project that transported Watts residents to high-employment areas. Within two years, other urban areas were also requesting such assistance. Upon taking over the RD&D program, Dr. Hemmes became particularly critical of this group of projects because of their nonrigorous methodology and social orientation. The director of the Civil Rights Office was encouraged to assume responsibility for managing these projects in his office, and eventually he agreed. Dr. Hemmes continued to criticize these projects. A substantial effort was devoted to improving the methodology used in the projects and to redirecting the emphasis toward developing new concepts and techniques that would improve service to transportation-disadvantaged groups such as the poor, handicapped, and elderly. There was and continues to be a strong demand for funds to support such projects by local communities, and the administrator felt it would be unwise to discontinue this effort.[11] However, the yearly funding has been held at a low level, and few people have been assigned to work on this type of project.[12]

As for Dr. Hemmes's preference for using RD&D to improve existing transit, this direction was never followed very far, because there was higher-level political interest in research on, and development of, new forms of urban transit. Secretary Volpe had a keen interest in developing new systems such as gravity vacuum trains, personal rapid transit, and tracked air cushion vehicles.[13] As of this writing, the White House has remained strongly interested in similar transit innovations.[14]

Political pressures in general, and particularly pressures from high-level administrators who wished to carry out their own ideas about the best direction for urban transportation research, have resulted in (1) relatively high R and D budgets, (2) less priority for the more mundane improvements in such things as rail-rapid cars, (3) a great deal of reprogramming of projects and funds, and (4) little opportunity to systematically evolve a concept from the idea stage, through research, development, test, and demonstration. The UMTA research budget climbed from approximately $20 million to $40 million, to $75 million, to $115 million under conditions that precluded good management. The author has witnessed the complete reprogramming of proposed current year projects three times in a ten-day period due to changing secretarial mandates. The result of the reprogramming was to cut 70 percent of the funds planned for improving the state-of-the-art of rail-rapid transit and to shift the funds to allow demonstration of a new transit system for which neither the concept nor the equipment had been first tested on the DOT test facility.[15]

Given the above conditions, PPB analyses were not used to make any of these fundamental policy decisions. Dr. Hemmes's office did submit material used in the spring preview and program proposal submissions. However, this material was used only to explain the intended program; there was no critical analysis. The biggest problem for the analyst was to keep the draft submission updated in light of the many reprogramming decisions being made continually, which had to be reflected in the spring preview or program proposal submissions.[16]

The New Systems Study

A close look at two major activities in the life of urban transportation research will illustrate precisely how policy decisions were made in this program during the period under consideration. The first of these, the New Systems Study, occurred in the early years when the program was still operating in the Department of HUD.

In 1966, Congress amended the Urban Mass Transportation Act of 1964 and required that a study be submitted to it in eighteen months. The section read:

(b) The Secretary shall, in consultation with the Secretary of Commerce, undertake a project to study and prepare a program of research, development and demonstration of new systems of urban transportation that will carry people and goods within metropolitan areas speedily, safely, without polluting the air, and in a manner that will contribute to sound urban planning. The program shall (1) concern itself with all aspects of new systems of urban transportation for metropolitan areas of various sizes, including technological, financial, economic, governmental, and social aspects; (2) take into account the most advanced available technologies and materials; and (3) provide national leadership to efforts of States, localities, private industry, universities, and foundations. The Secretary shall report his findings and recommendations to the President, for submission to the Congress, as rapidly as possible and in any event not later than eighteen months after the effective date of this submission.[17]

The required study, due in March 1968, was submitted in May. The reasons for delay in submission and the eventual impact of the study are significant for what they reveal about policymaking during the official period of PPB.

The New Systems Study was promoted by a few men and was primarily the idea of one congressman, Henry Reuss (D-Wisconsin). Henry Reuss was a member of the House Banking and Currency Committee, which oversaw legislation for HUD. Reuss knew that HUD, with William Hurd as the head of the Urban Transportation Administration, used the R and D legislation as a veiled subsidy for improving existing systems with present knowledge and hardware. Reuss believed the program should be managed to bring about a revolution in urban transportation, not merely to hold the line for the existing obsolescent systems.[18] An effort should be made, he felt, to break dramatically with the past[19] and to create new forms of transportation for the future. He also believed federal money should be used to spur innovation in the universities, in the community, and in industry.[20]

Congressman Reuss and his staff actively involved themselves in meetings and conferences concerning urban transportation. He had countless meetings with transportation experts and wrote several articles on the subject. He proposed legislation to Charles Haar, HUD assistant secretary in charge of several major programs, including urban transportation. Although HUD was initially neutral to the idea of the New Systems Study, Haar and the new people appointed to the department were enthusiastic about it.[21]

The 1966 hearing on the Johnson administration's urban development bill became the vehicle for passage of the desired legislation. Congressman Reuss played a minor role in the hearings, but in executive session he proposed the amendment that called for the New Systems Study. The amendment was drafted by Reuss's office staff with Haar's cooperation. Reuss's proposal was received sympathetically by his fellow Democrats and by two Eastern Republicans, Widnall and Dwyer.[22] It was included in the final committee bill, and it proved to be a minor item in the floor discussion. The bill was passed 236 to 127.[23]

On the Senate side of Congress, Senator Joseph Tydings (D-Maryland) was the key actor. Hearings were held, and testimony was given in favor of the New Systems Study.[24] The committee bill included the new systems provision. On the Senate floor, Senator Tydings defended the study; Senator Tower (R-Texas) questioned it on the grounds that it was a duplication of research effort. The bill was passed 65-18.[25]

Only one conference committee issue involved the funding of the study: the House version called for separate appropriations, while the Senate version called for use of existing authorization for RD&D. The conference committee recommended the Senate version. Tydings and Reuss were both on the conference committee, and they supported each other's favorite interest: Tydings supported the whole idea of the study, and Reuss supported Tyding's managerial and university training provision.[26] Congress passed the bill, and President Johnson signed S.3700 into law on September 8, 1966.[27]

Charles Haar, assistant secretary for metropolitan development in HUD, became the individual principally responsible for managing the study. Haar's philosophy of management was to acquire bright people, to give them similar assignments, and to evaluate the various solutions, using them to formulate a composite set of recommendations. He pursued that philosophy by bringing together an ad hoc group of eminent colleagues. In order to build Congressional support, Haar himself emphasized concentrating on the development of new hardware for existing systems and also entirely new systems development. He also sought input from outside the traditional transportation community. He therefore included aerospace, engineering, and consulting firms among the contractors, and he acquired some civil servants from the Department of Defense to manage the contracts.[28]

The HUD New Systems Study became a framework for three major studies. The first was to be a futuristic study of ideal technological solutions to the urban transportation problem that could be available in five to fifteen years. The second was to be a study of emerging new systems and significant improvements possible for existing urban transportation that could be available in three to eight years. The third was to be a study to find ways to obtain improved results from existing transportation technologies that could be available in six months to three years. Requests for proposals were sent, and eventually seventeen contractors were selected, among them many consultants not usually working in urban transportation.[29]

As the results of the studies became available and preliminary recommendations were made, the most obvious conclusion was that the solution to the transportation problem would have to involve both hard and software components; there was no one ideal solution.[30] A composite report had to be written in a very short period of time; it set out a $980 million, fifteen-year program.

What was the role of PPB in arriving at this significant policy recommendation? None whatsoever. The PPB staff in HUD had nothing to do with the study, and no attempt was made to incorporate it into the PPB submissions.[31] Considering the political mandate for this study and the nonuse of PPB on other policy matters in HUD, the nonuse of PPB is not surprising in this instance.

What was the effect of the New Systems Study on policy? None. Congressman Reuss, the key congressional impetus for the study and main actor in the process, had moved on to other interests, and there was no one to assume the legislative interest.[32] The bureaucratic reaction was also one of inaction. About this time, the Urban Transportation Administration was transferred to the new DOT and became the UMTA. The new administrator, Sitton, wanted an urban problem emphasis an immediate pay-off demonstration projects in cities. The next administrator, Villarreal, appointed by President Nixon, refused to follow the New Systems Study because it was a Johnson administration product.[33]

Tracked Air Cushion Vehicle

Secretary John Volpe came to the DOT as part of the Nixon administration in 1969. He brought a keen desire to begin and implement something new and exciting. This was particularly true in the field of ground transportation, in which there were many potential revolutionary breakthroughs in the idea stages but none that had progressed much beyond that point. Secretary Volpe was very interested in the gravity vacuum train concept and in the French tracked air cushion vehicle (TACV). After some preliminary work on the gravity vacuum train, the secretary and others in the Department concluded that the concept was prohibitively expensive to build.[34]

During his first months in office, however, Secretary Volpe also traveled to France and inspected the Aerotrain (a TACV). The secretary was impressed; upon his return to his department, he sent an aide to explore further the possibility of American research on the Aerotrain. The aide recommended that DOT should not contract with a French firm because of the adverse balance of payments situation at that time.

Rohr Corporation, a California aerospace firm, became interested in building the train and planned a joint venture with a French firm. The secretary liked the joint proposal and decided the department should conduct a demonstration of TACV with little R and D before the demonstration. The secretary was keenly interested in having an operating demonstration by October 1972. This deadline was always stressed by the secretary, with the added stipulation that the secretary and "other officials" could ride on the demonstration by October 1972.[35]

The problem then became one of site selection. Secretary Volpe favored the Washington, D.C. Dulles International Airport Access Route, but the undersecretary and others thought some alternative site might be best. A DOT task force was established to investigate sites, and ultimately the Los Angeles Airport-to-Palmdale site was recommended and was accepted by the secretary.[36]

From the beginning, it was felt that there must be a local sponsor and a local share. Los Angeles was selected primarily because the Los Angeles Department of Airports was very much interested in the project and had the necessary resources for the estimated local share. A technical study grant was made to Los Angeles for a detailed study of the cost, the proposed route, and technical problems. As a result of this detailed analysis, the cost estimate of the project escalated radically, from about $40 million to about $200 million. The secretary, possibly reacting cautiously because of the SST cost escalation at the time, set a ceiling of $50 million for the federal share.[37] The proposed Los Angeles TACV project produced an amazingly large number of complaints and many technical difficulties.

1. The route selected required the use of the center section of a major freeway, thus limiting construction to the early morning hours, and even then requiring $1.5 million for a temporary extra lane.

2. The demonstration would amount to only an eleven-minute ride from the San Fernando Valley and would drop off riders in a parking lot fifteen-to-twenty minutes away from the airline terminal. Therefore, a decision was made to also build an intra-airport transit system, adding $48 million to the original estimate.

3. Two preferred station locations proved to be almost impossible to acquire because of local opposition.

4. The route selected also ran into strong local political opposition because it coincided with the best route for a planned regional transit system. Local opposition became so strong that the state legislature voted to prohibit the use of the route for the TACV.

5. The airport's local share of the total cost became increasingly doubtful because (1) the local share increased from an estimated $20 million to $150 million; (2) the project put the airport into the business of airport access, which was opposed by the Air Transport Association; (3) the airport revenue needed to service the airport bonds was decreasing because of a depressed economy; (4) revenue from the TACV service was later forecasted as being half the original

estimate; and (5) it would hurt the longer-range project of a San Diego-Los Angeles-San Francisco high-speed ground transportation system.[38]

For the above reasons and others, Secretary Volpe realized that a Los Angeles TACV was not feasible and that the project should be allowed to die. He did not, however, lose interest in the TACV demonstration. Instead, he decided to build the TACV at Dulles as he had originally planned, and to announce this in his speech to the Washington Council of Governments (COG). This decision was made two weeks prior to the Februrary 16, 1971 COG speech, and a completion date of May 1972 was decided upon for the project.[39]

This Washington, D.C. project would link Dulles International Airport with a terminal point at Dolly Madison Boulevard, just east of the Capital Beltway. It was to consist of a single 13.5-mile guideway and one electrically powered vehicle capable of speeds up to 150 mph. This $22.3 million project was to be totally funded out of existing RD&D authorized funds, but in order to accomplish this, significant reprogramming of a program already approved by Congress was required. Thus, congressional approval was necessary.[40]

The Dulles site presented several advantages. First, DOT already owned the right-of-way. Second, the site would displace no one except at the Dolly Madison Terminal. Third, it would demonstrate the technology in limited actual usage. Fourth, it was argued that it could be extended to mesh with the planned regional transit system already under construction.[41]

No thorough analysis was done, and no effort was made to consider TACV as part of UMTA's "logical" RD&D effort. The secretary, largely influenced by the president of Rohr Corporation, decided that the technology was good, that it should be demonstrated, and that Dulles was the ideal site, especially in light of the International Air Exposition to be held at Dulles.[42] The secretary, being very busy, left the congressional liaison to others in the department.[43]

The role of congressional liaison is often overlooked. For members of the executive branch, it is an important ingredient in getting congressional approval for major undertakings. It was important at this time, because, as mentioned above, appropriation committee approval was necessary before DOT could start the demonstration. In the case of the Dulles TACV, two weeks were given for congressional liaison. While the secretary and undersecretary were traveling elsewhere, nine working days were used in trying to decide what the appropriate liaison was. Finally, on the Friday before the weekend speech, the UMTA administrator phoned all the key senators and congressmen available. As Hill watchers know, most senators and congressmen are not in their offices on Fridays, and proper liaison requires time. This "liaison" took less than four hours on the phone.[44]

Significant opposition came from Republican Representative Broyhill of northern Virginia. He was smarting under an earlier Volpe decision not to grant a sales tax to Arlington County for over-the-counter purchases at National Airport. The secretary had also strongly criticized Broyhill for advocating a monorail as a connecting link between Dulles and National Airports, and, finally, the department had allowed Democratic Senator Spong to announce the Dulles TACV project. Representative Broyhill opposed the reprogramming of RD&D funds in Congress and wrote a strong letter to the secretary in opposition. He questioned the propriety of the Rohr Corporation's lobbying strategy of offering free congressional trips to Paris to see a similar system; he noted the fact that the planned METRO could not use the Dulles access right-of-way if it were used for TACV, and he stated that the TACV would "provide nothing more than a carnival-type of amusement ride for fidgety children whose parents are waiting for a plane at Dulles."[45]

House hearings were held on March 23, 1971, and it was decided not to allow the reprogramming of RD&D funds.[46]

The secretary still did not abandon the concept of TACV; instead, he decided to pursue a more conventional R and D approach. The decision was made to develop the hardware first, test it at the DOT test facilities, and then proceed if all efforts proved that continuing R and D were merited. Both congressional appropriation committees approved this approach when funds were requested for what was now called the Urban TACV.[47]

RD&D Decision-Making

One obvious conclusion can be drawn from the above: PPB was not used as an aid to making decisions on urban transportation RD&D. The PPB process described in Chapter 2 assumed that the leadership in the department and in the department's major subunits would utilize PPB to make decisions and that major decisions on a program would occur roughly on a yearly cycle. When the secretary and others took a strong interest in UMTA's RD&D program, they were not interested in analysis of alternatives or long-range planning that might interfere with or delay the implementation of their decisions. In order to get a decision implemented quickly, administrators would often sacrifice systematic procedure. Consider the history of the TACV project just described.

At first, the TACV was not included in the budget appropriation; it was then programmed in RD&D; then it was shifted to the capital grant budget; then it was shifted back to RD&D with the Dulles decision; then it was eliminated entirely; and finally it existed as a less significant project. All of this occurred in a period of four months. At one time, the TACV effort would have taken up 40 percent of the then current year's RD&D budget.

The interjection of high-level officials into the decision-making process with no regard for the PPB process is illustrated by both TACV and the New Systems Study. Key congressmen, senators, the secretary, and others concerned themselves with RD&D policy without benefit of the PPB process. This situation continued with the Nixon White House stress on new systems transit demonstrations and with the secretarial initiatives on such things as Transpo 72.[48] Political considerations override staff work and long-range planning. This reality has been dramatically illustrated, and its significance should not be underestimated.

In fairness, it should be pointed out that the decision-making environment of RD&D in the Urban Mass Transportation Administration was somewhat unusual. First of all, urban transportation is a "glamour topic"; any accomplishment can easily gain publicity. The successful UMTA Shirley Highway Bus Demonstration project, for example, received national news coverage. The immediate and widespread attention that transportation projects can get makes the decisions involved in such projects more important politically than many other governmental decisions.

Another unusual factor in the decision-making environment was the ease with which a high-ranking politically appointed executive such as Secretary Volpe, who personally enjoyed this type of research anyway, could shape the program; other agencies in his department conducted research, but various legal requirements or other circumstances in these subunits precluded the possibility of his having a free hand in making decisions.

A very important and unusual circumstance was the great flexibility of RD&D program funds, owing primarily to the rapid expansion of the program over a short period of time.

Finally, new forms of transportation are a universally appealing subject—everyone travels. Many political executives and congressmen, even those not directly involved with policymaking in this area, such as Congressman Reuss, are attracted to this topic and have ideas about it which they would like to see tried out.

The PPB literature and official guidance would lead one to think that major shifts in R and D policy would be preceded by a special analytical study and be discussed in the program proposal; the department would use the program proposal as the background document and the official review of the program proposal would be the time for changing R and D policy. In reality, policy decisions were being made in reaction to a confluence of factors, including external political pressures, crises, biases of influential people, and such human characteristics as pride. This nonuse of PPB can be attributed to the very political nature of the subject; PPB ran counter to the political realities of the circumstances.

4 Urban Mass Transportation Subsidies

Since 1964, the federal government has had a grant-in-aid program addressed to subsidizing the urban transit industry. Since the beginning of this involvement in the nationwide urban transportation problem, government leaders have spent much time analyzing and debating possible solutions. This chapter discusses some of the decision-making situations that have occurred.

The Urban Mass Transportation Assistance Act of 1970

The Urban Mass Transportation Act passed in 1964 was amended in 1970 to provide authorization of $3.1 billion over a five-year period to upgrade, extend, improve, and develop new bus, rapid-transit, and commuter rail systems across the nation. In making the 1970 commitment, Congress stated that its full intention was to make a total of $10 billion available by 1982 for urban transit improvement. This increase in authorization was a great leap forward in federal assistance to urban transit from the previous levels of about $300 million per year.[1]

The events surrounding the passage and later implementation of this act illustrate another governmental decision-making process. The decision by executive branch officials to press for greater funds for mass transit occurred in 1968 in the last few months of the Johnson administration. Realizing the political mood of the time and the realities of presidential transition, key congressional supporters of mass transit and administration officials agreed to await the new president.[2] This proved to be a fortunate decision, because the new secretary, John Volpe, and one of his new assistant secretaries, James D'Orma Braman, became successful advocates of the legislation within the Nixon administration.[3]

Assistant Secretary Braman was formerly mayor of Seattle and had championed a new rapid-rail system for the Seattle metropolitan area. This background made Mayor Braman and his key aide, Michael J. Cafferty, strong, articulate, and knowledgeable promoters of transit. Moreover, both men were still active in the national transit scene, since Braman was the chairman of the League of Cities transportation policy committee. Upon assuming his new position as assistant secretary for environment and urban systems, Mayor Braman and Cafferty, his new deputy assistant secretary, started lobbying in DOT for more federal support of transit, particularly in the form of a trust fund for mass transit.[4] A trust fund is specifically earmarked authorized funds normally associated with a specific revenue source, such as, excise tax, to be used exclusively for a specific purpose. A good example is the Highway Trust Fund used to finance highway projects, which receives its funds from the gasoline excise tax.

Secretary Volpe shared Braman's thinking and endorsed the trust fund concept in March 1969 at the Pittsburgh Urban Transportation Conference. From March to the end of July, Braman and Volpe worked to sell the Nixon administration on the trust fund approach. They were unsuccessful, however, because the counselor to the president, Arthur Burns, and the Bureau of the Budget director, Robert P. Mayo, opposed any new trust funds at all. Such trust funds, they maintained, limit the president's ability to manage the economy by constraining his power to cut the budget. So the White House said "no" to the trust fund. It did, nevertheless, decide to aid mass transit significantly by advocating legislation that would increase the authorization level for transit.[5]

This White House decision was very important in terms of urban mass transportation, but it created difficulties with the transportation lobbies for Volpe and Braman. Braman eventually convinced the League of Cities that the trust fund was not critical and that the White House bill should be supported. Mayor Richard Daley of Chicago, then the most active mayor on the transportation issue, remained opposed to the White House proposal.

Braman, acting as negotiator between the administration and the urban lobby, next brought about agreement on using a five-year contract authority provision in the bill instead of simple authorization. (Contract authority permits an agency to obligate money without appropriation *unless* the appropriation committee puts a limit on the authorized money.) Volpe concurred in this and converted Senator Tower, a former foe of urban transportation legislation. Tower then assisted by rounding up GOP votes. Even Senator Thurmond (R-SC) supported the bill in spite of the fact that he was one of the most outspoken Senate opponents of the 1961 and 1964 urban transportation bills.[6]

The House presented a more difficult lobbying problem because of the contract authority provision. The House Appropriation Committee has long been a foe of contract authority, calling it "back-door spending." Eventually the urban transit lobby worked out a procedure under which Representative Boland, chairman of the Appropriation Subcommittee on Transportation, would accept the long-term contract authority.[7]

The urban transit lobby was led by the League of Cities and the US Conference of Mayors. Other members included the American Transit Association, the Institute of Rapid Transit, the Railroad Progress Institute, the Amalgamated Transit Union, the Laborers International Union, and the AFL-CIO.[8] John Gunther, executive director of the US Conference of Mayors, lobbied actively himself and hired Fred B. Burke to coordinate the transit lobby effort. (This action was quite unusual for the urban lobby group; the closest similar situation occurred when they hired former congressmen Albert Rains and

Lawrence G. Henderson to manage the creation of HUD.) Fred B. Burke was a former DOT deputy assistant secretary for public affairs and had worked on the Hill. For his work on the 1970 transit legislation he received $22,000 for thirteen months of work.

The lobby was described by Senator Richard B. Russell (D-Ga) as "the damndest coalition that I've ever seen," and one House Banking and Currency Committee staff member said it was "a letter-perfect lobbying job—one that ought to be put in the textbooks." The entire lobby cost $100,000 and was able to bring old opponents into the fold, resulting in votes such as 84-4 in the Senate. It brought officials from cities of various sizes from every section of the country to testify on behalf of the legislation. It also made full-fledged supporters of such stalwarts of the highway lobby as the General Motors Corporation, the American Association of State Highway Officials, the National Automobile Dealers Association, and the Automobile Manufacturing Association.

As mentioned above, one problem was to get the House Appropriation Committee to accept the use of contract authority. Representative Boland, chairman of the key appropriation subcommittee, eventually agreed to contract authority, but the "agreement" with Boland was fragile. The UMTA administrator, Carlos C. Villarreal, balked when it came to pledging to review with Boland the coming year's spending schedule. The administrator and his staff feared the possibility of a multibillion-dollar pork barrel with each project being justified individually. The lobby was displeased with the Nixon administration, because "UMTA doesn't realize that Boland holds most of the cards."[9] The whole problem proved not to be critical, however, once Boland and other key congressmen were shown a DOT-UMTA schedule for spending the money over the years.[10]

At this point, when cooperation among all who had agreed to support the bill was particularly important, a *National Journal* article described the lobbying effort.[11] The publication of the article completely split, for a time, the key actors in the urban transit lobby, because many thought Burke was given a disproportionate amount of credit. The White House was displeased with the *National Journal* article because it contained overtones that the bill was not really "bipartisan." This development almost proved disastrous.[12]

Meanwhile, the bill had progressed to conference committees; the House version provided for $5 billion contract authority and the Senate version for $3.1 billion. The leadership in the Office of Management and Budget had changed to George Schultz and Caspar Weinberger. Both of these men were hostile to the urban transportation legislation, and they were particularly displeased with the possibility of $5 billion contract authority. They argued that President Nixon should veto his own bill, especially if the Congress voted out a $5 billion bill.

The DOT made critical lobbying efforts at this time. It convinced the League of Cities, the American Transit Association (ATA), and others in the lobby group not to push for the $5 billion version. Representative Boland was persuaded to sponsor an amendment to the House version to lower the amount to $3.1 billion. This action effectively neutralized the Office of Management and Budget's objection and quieted White House fears.[13] The bill was passed, and President Nixon signed it into law on October 15, 1970.

A postscript on the law's implementation is enlightening in terms of follow-through on government decision-making. In subsequent years, Representative Boland's and Senator Stennis's appropriation subcommittees have inserted language into the appropriation bills that has effectively voided contract authority for each fiscal year. Also, these same committees have provided appropriation ceilings higher than those requested in the President's Budget with the expectation that once the appropriation bill becomes law, the Office of Management and Budget will probably impose an apportionment on the appropriation amount significantly less than the amount allowed by Congress. For example, the Congress provided a ceiling of $900 million in FY 1971, but OMB held down that amount to $600 million through its apportionment powers.[14] The appropriation committees have effectively negated "contract authority," and OMB continues to be hostile to the urban mass transportation program.

What part did PPB play in the passage of the 1970 Act and its subsequent implementation? The PPB staff, the DOT Office of Program Planning, did prepare the funding schedule demanded by Representative Boland and others, and the staff did prepare a draft of the House report on the bill. In later implementation on the act, the PPB staff did prepare the initial justification for the coming budget. It might be added here that the rationale they developed remained approximately the same throughout the planning and budgeting processes, although, as will be seen, it was not well received at OMB, which demanded better and more detailed justification as well as evidence of improved management within UMTA.[15]

Policy Questions

The problems of getting the Urban Mass Transportation Assistance Act of 1970 passed into law pale by comparison to the problems of making decisions about how to implement it. Since the passage of the 1970 legislation, policy on how properly to administer the program has been unsettled and a subject of much discussion in the executive branch. As mentioned earlier, UMTA had a capital grant program prior to the 1970 legislation, but the yearly appropriation was relatively small. The 1970 legislation opened the door for the federal government to invest billions of dollars in a few urban areas. The magnitude of the expenditure involved caused a great deal of concern at the White House and the

Office of Management and Budget primarily because of the significant impact it would have upon the national budget.

Congress authorized from the general revenue a total of $3.1 billion for FY 1971 to FY 1975. From this amount, all of UMTA's activities were funded. First priority in funding was given to (1) salaries and expenses, (2) the RD&D activity, (3) technical studies, (4) university research and training, and (5) capital grant assistance for bus transit in small and medium-sized communities. This de facto priority required a relatively small and fixed amount (in FY 1971 $200 million). The remaining amount was used for capital assistance for improvements and extensions of existing large transit systems (e.g., Chicago, New York) and capital assistance for new transit systems (e.g., Pittsburgh, Baltimore, Atlanta). This remaining amount varied each year from lows of about $200 million to higher amounts such as $400 and $800 million per fiscal year.[16]

Six urban areas (New York, Chicago, Philadelphia, Boston, Cleveland, and San Francisco) are particularly interested in improving and extending their rail-rapid and commuter services. Their problems are often acute. In 1971, 1300 rapid-transit cars at least thirty years old were still operating in the US; some were nearly fifty years old. In New York City, 1000 cars were nearing the end of their usefulness. At the time, estimates for new car replacements ranged from $250,000 to $400,000 per car. The East Boston (Revere Beach) service used forty-eight cars of 1923 vintage for rush-hour service. In Philadelphia, 140 cars were in generally very poor condition and were being poorly maintained because of inadequate equipment. New York, Chicago, Philadelphia, Boston, and San Francisco were considering extending or adding new lines to their systems.[17]

Sixteen urban areas (Atlanta, Baltimore, Buffalo, Dallas-Ft. Worth, Denver, Detroit, Honolulu, Houston, Kansas City, Los Angeles, Miami, Minneapolis-St. Paul, Pittsburgh, San Juan, Seattle, and St. Louis) are contemplating new transit systems. Atlanta, Baltimore, Buffalo, and Pittsburgh either now have or will likely receive federal assistance. These systems represent a need for over $1.5 billion.[18]

One policy question being debated in the executive branch is this: Should the federal government subsidize the construction of major new fixed transit systems at all? Several policy papers have been requested of UMTA's Office of Program Planning on this subject.[19] Even as the matter is being considered, UMTA is providing capital assistance for Pittsburgh, Baltimore, and Atlanta and is planning on funding Buffalo. The sums of money provided, except to Pittsburgh, are for the first phases of programs only, but some could argue the federal government has made a moral commitment to complete the projects. A subject not addressed which may also be significant is: Should new or old systems have priority on the limited amount of money available?[20]

What part did PPB play in this debate? One would expect from Chapter 2 that PPB would be used to decide policy on this subject. In this instance, the Office of Program Planning developed the position papers that were asked for.

Analyses and other material were presented in the spring preview and special analyses were requested as a result of the Departmental spring preview hearing. There is no evidence that these analyses contributed to a DOT policy, but they were a part of the policymaking process. In other words, PPB was used in this case as the means to consider policy changes.

Project Selection Criteria

Even if the government decided to subsidize the construction of major transit systems, it could not meet all the acceptable requests for entirely new systems.[21] Moreover, it felt that a much better management system should be developed before large expenditures would be justified.[22] In a February 1970 memorandum, therefore, Robert P. Mayo, director of the Office of Management and Budget, called for a special analytical study by UMTA on the topic "Program Plan and Evaluation Criteria for UMTA Program." It was due May 1, 1970. The "call" said in part:

In the absence of clear reasonable objectives and a financial and action plan, the new program can easily evolve into a first-come-first-served pipeline through which cities, competing for Federal funds, quickly submit proposals rather than take time to think through long term needs. Unless there are adequate criteria for evaluating capital grants and RD and D Applications and results, the Department will be unable to determine which projects are most cost effective in relation to the program objectives. It is recognized that because of the newness of the program, the end product of the study will be a first approximation which will need subsequent updating as additional knowledge and experience is [sic] gained. The study should propose specific mechanisms for achieving this updating.[23]

UMTA's Office of Program Planning was assigned the responsibility of developing the special study. Milton Brooks wrote the response, which was submitted to OMB June 30, 1970.

Chapter 1 described the UMTA programs and discussed the general problems of developing criteria for them.

Chapter 2 discussed criteria concerned with the characteristics and substance of individual projects as they were submitted for federal assistance.

Chapter 3 discussed criteria concerned with over-all objectives and general program strategy, allocation of resources to program and project areas, staging of the project review process, and methods for the comparison of projects for approval.

Chapter 4 stated a number of general conclusions concerning the selection of criteria for UMTA programs and identified areas for priority action.[24]

The reaction from the secretary's Office of Planning and Program Review and from the Office of Management and Budget was that the preliminary report was interesting but that they wanted, at least, a first approximation called for in Mayo's letter. Robert McManus, acting assistant administrator for program planning, was asked to develop the necessary information. By this time, Mayo's original broad request had been narrowed to the problem of developing criteria for the capital grant program.[25]

UMTA did have goals, objectives, and criteria, but they were a mixture of nonoperational phases and broad guides. The official goals and objectives were developed by the Office of Program Planning and they were, in summary:

The long-run goal of urban transportation is to provide users with safe, fast, convenient service as efficiently and economically as possible while representing and preserving other community objectives and values with urban areas.

Short-run goals, therefore, must necessarily be to continue and provide where necessary at least minimum public transportation for those who do not have access to private transportation for essential trips, and to foster improvements in coverage and frequency of service, safety, comfort, speed, convenience and efficiency without aggravating other basic urban problems.

The statement goes on to cite two more objectives:

1. Maintenance and Extension of Service Coverage of Public Transportation.
2. Improvements in Quality Public Transportation (a) For Users, (b) For Everyone.[26]

UMTA's Office of Program Operations used its own criteria and guide:[27] a prospective project had to meet minimum criteria established by law and applicants were grouped by those that provided support for (1) renewal of existing systems, (2) extensions of existing systems, and (3) new systems.[28] Projects were funded, if enough money was available, with priority given the first, then second groups. Large projects in the second group and the third group were considered sensitive decisions. The assistant administrator for program operations (William Hurd) counseled with the administrator and sometimes the secretary. Decisions were made on a case-by-case basis.[29]

Robert McManus (acting assistant administrator for program planning) prepared a new draft of the special analytical study requested by Mayo, and it was circulated among UMTA, DOT, and OMB key personnel on November 12, 1970. He was under a great deal of pressure from Deputy Director Weinberger (OMB) and Secretary Volpe to get the job done, as it was originally due May 1.[30] The draft was an attempt to logically draw together the goal and objectives statement of the Office of Program Planning, William Hurd's (Office of Program Operations) guides, and some more specific criteria as called for by OMB.[31] In addition, the draft also argued that there were two approaches to program administration: objective oriented or demand responsive. The implication was that UMTA was demand responsive.[32] The final report was sent December 17, 1970. It was substantially the same as the draft version, except that McManus had now altered the UMTA goals to read:

1. The provision of adequate mobility to these substantial segments of the urban population which may not command the direct use of motor vehicles.
2. The improvement in overall traffic and the reduction of time-in-travel about the urban regions in peak hours of travel demand; i.e., relief of congestion.
3. The achievement of land-use patterns and/or environmental conditions which effectively contribute to the physical, economic and social well-being of urban communities.[33]

Donald B. Rice, assistant director of OMB, proposed recommendations on the capital grant criteria on February 9, 1971. The recommendations were quite surprising:

1. place less emphasis on the concept of the "transportation disadvantaged,"
2. use 50 percent federal grant instead of 66 2/3 percent grant as a sanction for not meeting criteria, imposed by UMTA rather than being established by law,
3. force cities to "adopt at least one non-capital intensive means to reduce traffic congestion,"
4. include urban transportation as a part of special revenue sharing *and* still "press forward with the full development, implementation and use of comprehensive project selection criteria,"
5. request "that the Department . . . submit the revised, agreed to, criteria to the transit industry and to ACIR for comment and clearance by state and local government, per OMB Circular A-85, by February 22, 1971," and
6. require detailed data items and the use of scientific operating measures in the criteria.[34]

Villarreal, at the urging of McManus, reacted strongly to OMB's recommendations. He suggested that Undersecretary Beggs write a memorandum to Rice saying in part:

Certain issues are apparent which seriously involve the creditability of the Nixon Administration vis-à-vis the cities. We particularly are concerned about the diametrically opposite direction represented by the proposed criteria for UMTA and the proposed special revenue sharing legislation for transportation. It seems incredible that DOT would be announcing more specific criteria for UMTA programs at such a major junction in domestic program policy direction.

. . . we are deeply concerned that implementing the criteria without permitting more lead time to prepare the clientele of the program, and for UMTA itself to prepare, will immobilize program activity. Rather than leading the cities and transit authorities along, which takes some finesse, we appear to be clubbing them. They are already chafing under the reduced program level for the current fiscal year. But they certainly haven't been anticipating what they would consider further impediments to realizing the benefits of the new legislation—at least not in this fiscal year.[35]

In a February 17, 1971 memorandum to Rice, Undersecretary Beggs did argue the points suggested by Villarreal, but in a less emotional tone. He pointed out the apparent conflict in philosophy, the likely negative reaction of the cities, and the difficulty of imposing added information requirements. He concluded: "We believe the issue of announcing much tighter criteria for the UMTA program in the near future should be reconsidered."[36] Rice responded on March 15. Not only did OMB not concur with DOT's position, but Rice signaled an intent to implement more prescriptive criteria. He also suggested that OMB work with DOT and the Domestic Council in drafting the letter transmitting the criteria to the Advisory Commission on Intergovernmental Relations (ACIR).[37]

DOT finally incorporated the major changes recommended by OMB. Beggs, in a telephone interview with a *New York Times* reporter, pointed out that the Nixon administration was convinced some kind of criteria was needed. Possibly systems are needed in some cities, but it is questionable in others. Criteria are needed to help make those critical decisions.[38] Carlos Villarreal pointed out that perhaps twenty US metropolitan areas could have rapid-rail systems, but limited money would force a selection of only a few cities.[39] This fact was not a stated reason for the criteria, but it was always considered.[40]

On April 30, 1971, DOT transmitted the revised selection criteria to OMB. Beggs pointed out that this document should not be transmitted to the ACIR for the A-85 clearance process in that form, that a revised Information for Applicants was the correct form, and that he would submit a product in thirty days.[41] On June 29, 1971, Gordon Murray, assistant administrator for program planning, UMTA, formally transmitted the proposed revision of the Information to Applicants (which contained the new project selection criteria) to the Advisory Commission on Intergovernmental Relations. That letter formally requested that the consultation requirements of OMB Circular A-85 be used to inform state and local government associations of the proposed new guidelines.[42]

Representatives of the transit industry and the cities were taken by surprise. They were particularly concerned about the "unrealistic data demands and planning analyses" that would be imposed.[43] The American Transit Association, the Institute for Rapid Transit, and the National League of Cities-US Conference of Mayors believed that the new criteria "would have a devastating effect on the capital grant program." They believed that the effect of the guidelines would be to strangle the flow of funds by requiring endless justifications and elaborate rationales for projects that should be speedily considered and funded if urban mass-transit hopes were to survive.[44] William J. Ronan, president of the Institute of Rapid Transit (IRT) and New York State Transit Authority (MTA), was most upset about the criteria proposal. He argued that a disciplined approach to transit grant administration would be fine—when it also applied to highways and airports.

Fred Burke, who had lobbied for the 1970 transit legislation, was the consultant used by the transit industry and the cities to deal with urban transportation matters. He pointed out in an interview with this author that the industry and the cities heard about the new criteria the night before the June 22 DOT Urban Transportation Advisory Committee meeting. The first reaction was to feel DOT was guilty of a breach of faith because it did not consult informally prior to officially sending the document to ACIR. Circular A-85 does call for such informal consultation. He further pointed out that the cities and industry had a two-pronged response: negotiate with DOT for a very liberal use of technical studies money in order to build up local capacity to gather and provide desired data and drop the sanction for using less than two-thirds federal grant money for not meeting UMTA imposed criteria; and lobby Congress to mandate that DOT could not make grants for less than 75 percent of the project cost.[45] Senator Jackson (D-Wash.) voiced a similar concern to Secretary Volpe. Volpe responded by saying: "Your letter registered unwarranted alarm" and insisted that he supported transit. He stated that the industry was briefed, and he himself had talked to "industry public interest groups on July 8." He also pointed out that there would be a "full-fledged, bona fide consultation process with the industry."[46]

During the next few months, Robert McManus of DOT met with Burke to carry out that consultation process. The process was influenced by several parallel events. First, OMB held UMTA funds down to $600,000,000 from a congressionally allowed $900,000,000. For this the Nixon administration received a great deal of adverse reaction, both from industry and from Congress. Second, the transit operating subsidy proposal, (discussed later in this chapter) was being aired, with the Nixon administration against it and Congress favoring it. Third, the Single Urban Fund proposal, which would use Highway Trust Fund money for mass transit, was announced by DOT.

The industry and the cities did not like the selection criteria because they meant less money for major transit systems. Burke worked hard to soften points in the selection criteria that the industry did not like and sought assurances of the availability of planning grants to develop the DOT-desired information.[47] McManus worked with Rodger Atkins in the OMB, explaining the industry point of view and seeking OMB concurrence on the compromise positions as they evolved.[48]

The long A-85 process ended in May 1972. McManus felt that through the consultation and negotiation process, the administration had come as close as possible to the positions of industry and public interest groups. He did not expect the National League of Cities-US Conference of Mayors to protest the product, although he thought that ATA and IRT might not be satisfied. All parties, the public interest groups and OMB, thought the next steps of research and other aspects of implementing the criteria were critical. The public interest groups were slow in responding, so the final criteria, that is, Information to Applicants, was not published until early June 1972, becoming effective July 1, 1972. One critical event had occurred by this time: the 1972 housing bill was well on its way to passage, and it contained a provision that would have eliminated the possibility of varying the federal share under any criteria.[49]

Upon the request of OMB, the DOT Office of Planning and Program Review stipulated on March 21, 1972 that UMTA was to develop a "program issue" on implementing the project selection criteria. The paper was due for the departmental spring preview session on June 19, 1972.[50] This author and Robert McManus prepared the desired material. A draft of the revised internal procedures manual was provided to William Hurd. Mr. Hurd took strong exception to the proposed criteria. In fact, he did not even allow McManus to brief the Office of Program Operations staff on the new criteria they were to use. Hurd was at retirement age, and he decided to retire partially because of the shift in policy on his program.

At the June 19 meeting, a two-year research effort was announced, which meant that the criteria could be fully operational within two years. Undersecretary Beggs pointed out that the Nixon administration felt very strongly about these criteria and announced that President Nixon would probably veto the 1972 Housing Act, which contained a provision limiting the use of the new criteria. Beggs was particularly concerned about the provision in the legislation that would prevent the criteria from being used to lower the federal share on less "satisfactory" projects.[51]

What part did PPB play in developing the new project selection criteria? PPB was *the* instrument used by OMB to force DOT and UMTA to revise the selection criteria in the UMTA capital grant program. OMB established a special analytical study focused on changing the capital grant criteria, demanded that the study be done, took exception to it until UMTA adopted a new policy in line with OMB thinking, and insisted that the new criteria be made operational.

Transit Operating Subsidy

One section of the Urban Mass Transportation Act of 1970 called for a DOT study on the feasibility of federal assistance for urban mass transportation operating costs.[52] Congress was apprehensive about an operating subsidy, but some members (Senators Percy and Williams and Representative Koch) were very interested in such a proposal and had suggested specific legislation.[53] The Nixon administration and the Congress stated that legislation should not be considered until after DOT completed the feasibility study called for in the legislation. The report was due in October 1971.[54]

Milton Brooks in the Office of Program Planning was assigned the responsibility of preparing the report to Congress. One staff member, Arthur Spengler, and two consulting firms gathered the necessary information and prepared the analyses. The initial draft report, which was finished in October, was very critical of the transit industry and the operating subsidy concept. It pointed out the unreliability of the data gathered and the difficulty in drawing conclusions, and recommended a research effort to try to determine the best kind of subsidy program.[55] The report was circulated around the department and informally circulated to the transit industry.[56] Neither the secretary nor any other appointed official took an active part in these early stages of the report except to insist that the study be done on time.[57]

On September 4, 1971, Secretary Volpe, speaking at ceremonies in Boston, had opposed operating subsidies to transit on the grounds that they rewarded poor business practices. This was the first public clue as to the conclusions being reached in the first draft. The October draft came up with a brusque "no" verdict. William J. Ronan, a Rockefeller appointee to the New York State Metropolitan Transportation Authority, led the industry's opposition to the draft report.[58]

Ronan got Volpe to order a review of the draft and hold up its transmission to Congress. He argued that he represented a loyal Republican governor, that New York had a serious problem, and that he had to work with a Democratic senator because he could not get a sympathetic hearing from his own administration.[59] The major conclusions of the final report as they ultimately went to the Congress were:

- The transit industry is in a critical condition by any measure—declining ridership, deteriorating service, increasing costs, escalating fares, large operating deficits.
- In the short run, transit deficits merely reflect the policy choices of the community concerning fares and service, with a subsidy covering the difference.
- In the long run, transit has been adversely affected by policies favoring the automobile and encouraging auto oriented sprawl, and by the lack of coordinated local planning and zoning.
- Changes in these policies and experimentation with improved and responsive transit services could make transit a viable alternative in our conclusion and perhaps even make it self-sufficient.
- An operating subsidy in and of itself will not alleviate any of these underlying difficulties.
- Federal operating subsidies could be provided in a number of ways—but each mechanism raises a number of serious issues [such as:]
  a. How to judge need? What (or whose) objective should be served? Holding the status quo, improving service, helping the poor, or just relieving the financial strain of state and local governments.
  b. How to preserve incentives for efficiency?
  c. How to encourage institution and policy changes and improved service?
  d. How much surveillance and control?

The Report recommended:

a. Enactment of Transportation Revenue Sharing, as a way of increasing local
   initiative and flexibility in the use of Federal funds now going into
   transportation, allowing them to be used for transit operating subsidies if that
   is considered a priority need, and General Revenue Sharing, as a way of
   increasing the overall flow of Federal funds to state and local governments to
   meet needs in accordance with their own priorities.
b. Continuing evaluation of service and policy innovations that might improve
   transit and of the question concerning operating subsidies. Continue existing
   capital assistance and RD&D programs.[60]

The report's analyses were essentially the same as those in the earlier draft,
but consultation in the department, with the industry, and with OMB did make
a difference. The industry, working again through Fred Burke, got the report to
(1) admit a need, (2) admit a federal responsibility, (3) admit that some solution
was possible, and (4) take out negative comments directed toward the capability
of the transit industry. They believed this would allow them to argue to the
Congress that the only real question was selecting a mechanism.[61] OMB's major
concern was the additional money the draft report recommended for the
research program; therefore, such a program was not recommended, and
reference was made to using the knowledge gained from existing capital
assistance and research projects.[62] Due to his travel schedule, Volpe did not take
an active part in this matter at this time, and Beggs decided to take the hard line
preferred by OMB.[63]

Congress and the industry were not pleased with the report. In January,
Ronan persuaded Volpe to meet with subsidy lobbyists. They argued that (1) a
subsidy based on ridership would reward productivity, (2) the need at the local
level was severe, (3) the issue was out of political control already, and (4) some
types of subsidy would be passed anyway. Volpe then became a reluctant
champion of operating subsidies and ordered a high-level departmental task force
to come up with a subsidy program. This split the Nixon administration
position, since OMB remained hostile to the idea.[64]

A task force was established on December 17, 1971, with a mandate to have
its report to the secretary one month later. McManus was designated as chairman
and Brooks was part of that task force.[65] In January, the task force submitted a
"Discussion Paper: Alternative Programs of Federal Operating Grants for Mass
Transit," which analyzed further the possible mechanisms and problems of
providing operating subsidies. The paper suggested three alternative operating
subsidy programs.[66] In February, the task force completed its "Alternative
Programs of Federal Operating Grants for Mass Transit," an expansion of the
discussion paper that detailed the alternative programs.[67]

The transit lobby was also active during this period. In June 1971, the lobby
was internally debating what should be done.[68] In late December, the lobby

forces started to work together, and by January a compromise solution was achieved. Briefly it was:

- —Amend Section 3(a) of the capital program to allow grants for operating subsidy,
- —Recommend using ridership as a subsidy unit, thus encouraging greater productivity and defusing the inefficiency argument,
- —Admit it was not a perfect solution *but* that the need cannot be ignored,
- —Emphasize local communities cannot meet the need,
- —Argue that DOT could use impounded capital grant money already appropriated but not obligated due to OMB action,
- —Argue that small states and cities will receive significant and needed assistance,
- —Seek labor support,
  Admit that the program would help rich suburbs (an incentive to suburban Republicans to support the legislation), and
- —Point out that this action would aid the environment.[69]

The transit lobby was quite similar to the one that piloted through the 1970 legislation. Leadership roles went to Fred Burke (a free-lance lobbyist), Senator Harrison A. Williams (D-N.J.) and his aide Stephen J. Paradise, Chicago Mayor Richard J. Daley, and William J. Ronan of New York. Hand-picked medium- and small-town mayors and transit officials also were important members, and transit officials played a more significant role than in 1970. The key trade groups involved were the American Transit Association (Robert Sloan, executive secretary; and Carmack Cochran, president), IRT (Robert M. Coullas, executive secretary and Ronan, president), and the Railway Progress Institute. And, of course, the National League of Cities-US Conference of Mayors played a key role in the lobbying.[70]

The action on transit operating assistance started moving with force when Senate hearings were being held. Some comments reported in the *Washington Post* reflect the nature of the testimony given:

"At the end of the summer, our bus service will grind to a halt," John C. Baines, chief executive official of publicly owned Bi-State Transit, St. Louis, told the Senate Housing and Urban Affairs Subcommittee. "That's what you call a serious situation. We can't survive without operating assistance," Baines said. Bi-State, which serves an area with 1.5 million people, faces an operating deficit of $2 million and a total deficit of $5 million, including payments on the system's debt, Baines declared.

Cormack Cochran . . . said his privately owned transit company in Nashville, Tenn., has notified the city that it will have to cease operation this year because of deficits. . . . "We could not exist out of the fare box if we were given the unlimited power to raise fares."[71]

At those hearings, Cincinnati's mayor, Thomas A. Luken, pointed out why cities could not provide the needed subsidy: "Transit . . . in our metropolitan area ... is dying a slow death, and there is precious little time left." He emphasized that Cincinnatians already pay high local city fares and that the city is "in no position to meet a steadily worsening transit situation." To reinforce the small- and medium-sized city demand for the legislation, Mayor Sylvio Dupuis (Manchester, New Hampshire) and Senator Thomas J. McIntyre (D-N.H.) said: "Old and unattractive equipment, rising fares, rising maintenance costs, increasing operating costs and yearly deficits are combining with declining numbers of passengers to threaten the collapse of the privately owned bus line in my city. . . . Manchester needs help now."[72]

The result in the Senate was a victory for transit. The Senate Banking and Urban Affairs Subcommittee voted to grant an operating subsidy. It also voted to raise the federal share of capital grants to 90 percent. The Senate had voted for a transit operating subsidy once before, in 1970; however, it was blocked by the House, which wanted to see the results of the DOT study first.[73]

Meanwhile, the DOT was considering alternative methods of operating subsidy. The desire was to devise a plan that would tie the federal aid to improvement of service and put emphasis on efficient operations. The major obstacle was transit unions. The department wanted some kind of limitation on the subsidy involving labor costs, and granted this was a difficult problem to solve.[74]

Congressional action on the subsidy question increased in February and March. House hearings opened on the legislation on February 23. The transit lobby was advocating four positions: (1) a federal aid program of operating assistance, (2) a parity between transit and highway programs as to the federal matching ratio of funding, (3) an adjustment in the requirements necessary to receive grant assistance, and (4) an updating of the authorization and contract authority levels. Testimony given at the Senate hearing was repeated in similar form at the House hearing, but the lobbyists added an attack on the planning requirement and the OMB action which limited obligation to transit to $1 billion rather than the $1.5 billion appropriated by Congress.[75]

On March 1, a new antisubsidy threat developed in the Senate as Senator Allott (R-Colo.) decided definitely to offer a floor amendment to strike the program from the 1972 housing bill. Senator Sparkman (D-Ala.) and the Senate leadership decided to bring up the bill for floor action on March 2. This caused confusion in the transit lobby as they had anticipated a mid-March action and were not geared up for the earlier effort.[76] The amendment was, however, defeated by a 53-26 vote after a floor debate. Allott argued that the legislation did not set up a separate fund for operating expenses, and that the provision would drain away resources from the capital grant program. Senator Jacob Javits (R-N.Y.) countered with an amendment that added $400 million a year to the program, thus covering funds needed for operating expenses.[77]

The subsidy legislation, in the form of an amendment to the 1972 HUD Act, would amend the Urban Mass Transportation Assistance Act of 1964. It would provide for an operating assistance grant program with $800 million authorized for this purpose, and change the grant formula to a 90-10 ratio.[78]

Meanwhile, the House committee was considering legislation that would, among other things:

1. provide for an operating assistance reflecting the number of revenue passengers;
2. require a "comprehensive mass transportation service improvement plan";
3. stipulate a provision similar to the Javits amendment;
4. fix the grant at 80 percent of the net project cost, thus preventing the use of the project selection criteria as a means to lower a grant; and
5. increase the authorization to $6 billion instead of $3.1 billion.[79]

The *National Journal* pointed out the dynamics of the situation:

Representative Benjamin B. Blackburn, R-Ga, an activist member of the subcommittee with a conservative voting record, summed up the changing attitude in the House:

"It's a sorry state when we have to have Federal operating subsidies for mass transit.

"They will be like seduction: easy to start but hard to stop.

"Yet what alternative do we have? The companies are all going broke."[80]

On April 7, 1972, Volpe argued to John Ehrlichman, of the White House Domestic Council, and George P. Shultz, the director of the Office of Management and Budget:

The Administration should take the initiative before it is altogether too late. The President may soon be confronted with the equally unacceptable alternatives of having to sign a Democratic bill which simply dishes out funds and incorporates no incentives for improving transit services or vetoing the Housing Bill, thus appearing to be against assistance to the cities, elderly, handicapped, and other disadvantaged groups.

He argued that a crisis did exist in the transit industry with deficits up and ridership down. He argued, however, that there was a basis for optimism if transit improvements were effectuated in a coordinated way, as in Atlanta. He then advocated a specific operating assistance program, including a subsidy.[81] The Executive Office did not concur with Volpe.

Prior to this, Volpe had declined to testify to Congress,[82] but now the Nixon administration position was established and the tactics for dealing with Congress changed. DOT decided not to make a frontal attack on the operating subsidy issue. It reasoned that it had concluded sensitive negotiations with the transit lobby on project selection criteria and cooperated on sharing views on the subject of operating subsidy. McManus and others thought this good will was important and that "rising to the high ground of advocating the Administration's philosophy on revenue sharing combined with the Single Urban Fund proposal was far superior."[83] On June 13, 1972, the Nixon administration called for a deletion of the transit provision to the Housing Act amendments before the House Banking and Currency Committee. As explained earlier, the Housing Subcommittee had already approved the amendments, and now the matter was before the full committee. Secretary of HUD, George Romney, said the Nixon administration opposed the transit amendments and preferred funding transit through a Single Urban Fund. He also suggested that the proposed General Revenue Sharing plan would supply sufficient funds at the local level to meet the needs of transit operating costs.[84]

What part in this decision-making process did PPB play? If one were to be perfectly accurate, the answer would be none, in that this series of events fell outside of the PPB process. Actually, however, the decision-making process did involve the PPB process, because some of the critical actors were also involved in PPB for the Urban Mass Transportation Administration. The mandated congressional study was treated like a special analytical study except that the ultimate receiver was Congress. The events, after the study was submitted, were handled similarly to the project selection criteria. In many ways, it was a PPB study for UMTA.

Transit Subsidy Decision-Making

Unlike the decisions made on urban transportation RD&D (Chapter 3), PPB was used as an aid in making critical decisions on transit subsidies.

1. The PPB staff supplied important information needed in order to pass the 1970 legislation and they contributed input to the formal rationale for the Act.

2. Analyses and position papers were developed on the important question of the federal government subsidizing the construction of major transit systems.

3. The new project selection criteria was developed as a direct result of a special analytical study.

4. The policy debate surrounding a transit operating subsidy involved, to a significant extent, the PPB staff of UMTA.

In matters relating to policy on transit subsidy, the Office of Program Planning was the group considered responsible for developing initial analyses and recommending policy positions for DOT. Obviously, other groups and persons eventually had a great deal of influence on the policy as it finally evolved, but the PPB unit was a part of the policymaking process. In UMTA, neither Villarreal, the administrator, nor William Hurd, assistant administrator for program operations, took an active role in policy matters. Villarreal preferred to delegate the responsibility to the Office of Program Planning, and Hurd took very strong exception to the policy changes being forced upon his program, but decided not to bother about it. In DOT, there was a reluctance by other units to draft analyses and positions on these topics. Those units, such as the Office of Planning and Program Review, preferred to comment upon UMTA's position rather than work on the key policy questions *de novo*. The secretary himself had no strong predispositions on the subject of transit subsidy, and he became actively involved in policy matters only when early drafts of the DOT report on operating subsidies became controversial in the industry. OMB had strong predispositions on this subject, but its method of operation is such that it normally cannot draft the initial recommended policy position but can only shape the policy after some other group has prepared the first "draft." This left the Office of Program Planning with a meaningful role in shaping policy on transit subsidies; however, as noted earlier in this chapter, many groups ultimately had significant influence on the final policies that emerged.

What were the factors shaping decisions on transit subsidy policy questions? There was an awareness by the Nixon administration that a great deal of public money was at stake, and they had a desire to limit the amount spent. This is evidenced in the real possibility of Nixon vetoing his own 1970 legislation because the authorization was about $2 billion more than he asked for, the cutting out of a proposal that a large research effort be undertaken in connection with a transit operating subsidy, and the significant apportionment powers by OMB on UMTA appropriations. Another factor was the impressive lobbying effort mounted by the transit lobby group. The marshalling of a balanced set of witnesses to demonstrate that the transit problem existed in medium and large communities is one illustration of that excellent effort. The tremendous scope and complexity of the problem itself was an additional factor. Almost everyone eventually concurred that it was a serious national problem, but how to solve that problem continued to perplex congressional and executive branch decision-makers.

Strong personalities also were a vital factor. Secretary Volpe's and Mayor Braman's strong advocacy of the 1970 legislation was essential to the eventual passage of the law. The forceful pressure by OMB to have the project selection criteria implemented was critical, as it is very doubtful that it would have existed without such strong OMB pressure extending over a period of years.

One interesting contrast remains to be pointed out. Policy analysis, as conducted by UMTA's Office of Program Planning, played a major role in the public policymaking process with regard to transit subsidy matters, but none in terms of urban transit research. Why the difference? Although both subjects are extremely complex, there was a feeling among the decision-makers that disturbing fundamental questions regarding transit subsidy needed answers or further exploration before they, the decision-makers, were ready to make far-reaching policy. They wanted analysis to aid them in making their decision. The key decision-makers in urban transportation research, on the other hand, felt that they had the fundamental answers and that further study would simply obstruct their planned research. Both sets of circumstances were highly political, but there was a felt need for policy analysis to aid the decision-maker on transit subsidy matters, and no such need was felt in terms of urban transportation research. One might argue that policy analysis was appropriate in both sets of circumstances, but the key decision-makers involved did not feel the necessity for such analysis in both cases. The preconceived attitude toward the usefulness of policy analysis by those who influence and make policy is apparently significant in explaining the role of policy analysis in public policymaking.

5 Aids to Navigation

The United States Coast Guard took quite seriously the presidential order to develop a PPB system. During the author's tenure at the DOT, various conversations on PPB included praise for PPB as used in the Coast Guard. The Aids to Navigation program, for example, was a major Coast Guard effort and involved a set of recent major policy changes. These changes were made in the context of PPB.

Background

Aids to navitation is considered part of the "bread and butter" work of the US Coast Guard. It comprises about 20 to 25 percent of the Coast Guard budget each year. These various activities became Coast Guard responsibilities over a period of years. In 1939, the Lighthouse Service was transferred to the Coast Guard with all of its audio-visual aids to navigation and servicing equipment, such as, buoy tenders, buoys, lights, and also depots to service the equipment.[1] Then, during World War II, the Massachusetts Institute of Technology's Radiation Laboratory (part of the National Defense Research Committee) developed Loran A as the first major radio aid to navigation. The Coast Guard was selected as the service to operate the system. After the war, the system was expanded to include civil use.[2]

Two other radio navigation aids are also run by the Coast Guard. The Department of Defense developed Loran C in the late 1950s, and in 1970 the Navy developed the Omega system.[3] The Navy, however, still maintains a major interest with Omega, because Navy appropriations are used to run the system. The Coast Guard is the US operating agent of the Omega transmitting system as well as its world coordinator.[4]

In the mid-1960s, the Coast Guard became increasingly concerned about block obsolescence and the rapidly deteriorating condition of its aids to navigation equipment. The 1942-45 audio-visual aids required replacement, but modernizing was expensive. A single base used to service this equipment cost between $2 and $20 million.[5] Also, there was increasing awareness that the radio aids needed improvement.[6]

The Coast Guard initiated a quick study on the problem of buoy tenders, and the study team concluded that the equipment could be used more effectively by diverting three buoy tenders to oceanographic research, then a Coast Guard responsibility. The study was accepted by headquarters and field personnel. This success provided the internal confidence to take the logical step of reexamining the whole subject of aids to navigation.[7]

A special staff, the ad hoc National Navigation Plans Staff (composed of Lt. Commander Rosie and Captain Pohle and eventually including Captain Starley and Commanders Putski, Brower, and Glass) reporting to the chief of operations was created.[8] This study group was established in 1967, prior to the existence of PPB in the Coast Guard [9] It focused on two subjects: audio-visual aids and radio navigation aids. This staff created the planning documents that explained the rationale for the Coast Guard's shift in policy on aids to navigation.[10]

Planning for Audio-Visual Aids

Commander Putzki had the lead responsibility for audio-visual aids. Contractors were used extensively; Geonautics did a preliminary study for $85,000, and Booz Allen Applied Research conducted a detailed study for $250,000. Commander Putzki was then transferred, and Commander Brower became lead person on this activity. A National Bureau of Standards study was also done.[11] The key Booz Allen report recommended:

1. many more plastic buoys could be used instead of the traditional metal buoys;
2. in many situations less expensive floating aids could be used instead of the traditional and more expensive fixed aids;
3. lights rather than buoys should be used in shallow water (less than twenty-five feet);
4. small high-speed crafts could be effectively used to service aids;
5. the service force used to maintain the aids could be reduced, as the longer life and lower maintenance of the proposed new equipment would permit better service scheduling;
6. a cadre of trained and experienced aids to navigation personnel equipped with new, fast aids to navigation servicing boats should be established; and
7. the size of the service bases could also be reduced due to the new policies.[12]

Commander Brower actively monitored the contractors and did not accept all of the findings. For example, the original recommendation was to buy new servicing boats, but instead a decision was made to revitalize existing boats. The rationale was that, in three to ten years, research and development would probably produce a significant breakthrough in buoy tenders. Since new boats have a life expectancy of thirty years, it was judged best to use revitalized boats until the advanced boats were available.[13]

Senior headquarters and field officers remained reluctant to accept the recommended audio-visual changes. But both Brower and Putzki had taken every opportunity to brief Coast Guard groups on findings and recommendations as they were developed. After the passage of about one year and extensive briefings, the report was generally accepted in the Coast Guard.[14]

When the ad hoc National Navigation Plans staff was dissolved, the aids to navigation project manager requested Commanders Glass and Brower to be assigned to him. Like other military officers, Coast Guard officers serve a tour and are then routed to other responsibilities. The project manager had to argue his request at the division level in personnel, but he was successful. He pressed his claim because he wanted some continuation in aids to navigation from the planning stage to the more detailed program development stage.[15]

Planning for Radio Navigation Aids

The primary and more complex mission of the National Navigation Planning (NNP) unit related to electronic or radio navigation aids. When the DOT was established, the Office of Telecommunication in DOT was assigned the responsibility for "providing coordination and leadership on the Department's National Plan for Navigation"; it was also instructed to update that plan yearly.[16] The Coast Guard, as part of the new department, prepared the bulk of the plan.[17]

In May 1970 the first NNP was issued. It was the first updated statement of government policy on radio navigation since 1948. It represented an authoritative guide upon which civil users of radio navigation could base their decisions about purchasing radio navigation equipment. For example, a fishing boat owner would not wish to invest several thousand dollars in electronic equipment that either might be phased out or might never become the major electronic aid to navigation system. The NNP gives the boat owner the official government position on this subject so that he can make a wise investment decision.[18]

A careful examination of the 1970 NNP reveals a document that narrows its scope to civil air and marine interests primarily. It excludes consideration of air terminal navigation aids, marine audio-visual aids, and military navigation systems. The document discusses the system requirements for various air and marine uses and describes alternative system characteristics.[19] The plan did not take a position, in its discussion section, on which navigation system would be *the* system.

Several systems were considered in the plan, but some were more serious contenders. Loran A, developed during World War II, was the system used extensively by the civil air industry for transoceanic flights and by major civil maritime interests. Its transmission tolerance and accuracy are not satisfactory considering the higher standards that will be essential in the near future. Because it is used so extensively, Loran A still was a candidate, but to provide the necessary added coverage, the existing chains would have to be expanded.[20]

Loran C existed to meet military requirements, and it had the high-accuracy characteristics to meet future radio navigation needs. The utility of the system for general civil use was limited by the cost, complexity, and historic unreliability of the receivers.[21]

Decca, a British company and subsidiary of International Telephone and Telegraph, had built a system that was a prime candidate. The Decca radio navigation system was used primarily in northern Europe, southeastern Canada, the Persian Gulf, India, East Pakistan (now Bangladesh), South Africa, and Japan. Two temporary experimental chains were installed for civil use in the United States, one in New York and the other in California. The system could be established in the United States and provide what Decca called "the most accurate service where it is most needed." There would, however, be a problem of mutual interference with the Department of Defense Loran C stations.[22]

Omega was a recent development with great potential, although as the plan pointed out: "Whether or not this potential is realized is dependent on the impact of the lane resolution and propagation anomaly problems."[23]

The policy position to be taken by DOT on this matter was significant not only to the public who used radio navigation aids but also to the manufacturers who would stand to gain or lose significantly from the DOT decision. Another group with a stake in the decision were the technical people who came to believe "in their system." In fact, there was much input from advocates of one or another system.[24] Prior to the 1970s no decision on radio navigation was necessary, but increasing maritime traffic in the coastal confluence areas has forced the need for a government decision; "maritime traffic lanes" must be narrowed to allow for only a quarter-mile tolerance for error instead of the former tolerance of two to four miles.[25]

Decca-ITT was quite aggressive in its advocacy. Company officials had "*many, many* discussions" with everyone in DOT who would talk with them. They would set up demonstrations and cite their northern European experience.[26] Everyone this author interviewed pointed out Decca's advocacy. The company lobbied indirectly by renting their equipment to fishermen at a very low rate and encouraging them to write their congressmen and others saying that the Coast Guard should choose Decca. They advertised in trade journals and met with department officials such as Undersecretary Beggs on several occasions. One interviewee said: "They made it clear that they were friends with President Nixon."[27] Another interviewee, however, stressed that the extensive advocacy by the company played no part in the DOT final decision, which ultimately was delayed for over two years.[28]

Another strongly advocated system was Omega. Companies like Tracor, Inc., who built Omega equipment under Navy contract, advocated this system. They lobbied much as Decca did.[29] One interviewee cited a demonstration in the Atlantic involving Omega and Loran C equipment that showed Omega as the better system. Subsequently, the Omega operator admitted that they had not hooked up the Loran receiving antenna and had used unreasonably sized receiving equipment.[30] Several interviewees pointed out that officials in the Navy were particularly interested in the Omega and "advocated" the Omega system.[31] One interviewee stated flatly that no Navy officials advocated Omega.[32]

One interesting aspect of the advocacy for Omega was that the White House Office of Telecommunication took a strong position in favor of Omega. Everyone interviewed mentioned this. Why should this office advocate any one system? In each instance, the response was that a key developer of Omega who worked for the Navy had been hired by the White House and had continued his advocacy in his new position.[33]

The Coast Guard recommended Loran C to the department but on the condition that a low-cost reliable receiver be developed. The Coast Guard felt that Loran A was technically inadequate and the Omega had potential but had far too many technical limitations. Decca was technically inferior, they found; Loran C was the best if the receiver problem could be solved.[34] The department was not satisfied with the Coast Guard's recommendation, and more analysis was requested.[35]

The Coast Guard then initiated two significant actions. First, it contracted to develop a low-cost Loran C receiver. Two such receivers were developed by Coast Guard contractors. The industry, including Decca, independently developed four or five receivers at the expense of the companies. Second, in September 1971 an outstanding contractor was hired to evaluate the alternative systems. He subcontracted to "system advocates" for each of the three systems and told them to make the best case for their system. He also hired an independent evaluator, and he and the evaluator separately reviewed the "arguments." The final draft report was submitted to DOT in August 1972, and the contractor's conclusion was that Loran C was *the* desirable system.[36]

In April 1972, the second National Plan for Navigation was issued. In the Letter for Promulgation, Secretary John Volpe said: "A decision is expected to be made by the end of 1972 as to the navigation system to be utilized in the coastal/confluence zone." The plan was very similar to the 1970 version, except that it clearly spelled out that Loran A was out of the race.[37] Unofficially, Decca was no longer a contender, and a new version of Omega called Differential Omega was being considered. The decision, however, was to be postponed until the Coast Guard study was completed.[38]

PPB Applied

Every Coast Guard interviewee pointed out that the PPB process set out in the Coast Guard *Manual* was followed in the decision-making on aids to navigation and also that the various policy changes were made using the PPB system.[39] The system was briefly explained in Chapter 2, but a more elaborate explanation in terms of aids to navigation is provided here. In reviewing these steps it must be remembered that the focus is not only upon a policy change but also upon specific appropriations for the next budget year. A plan involving audio-visual or radio navigation aids consists of several budget authorizations and several Coast Guard "programs," such as R and D, as well as aids to navigation. Thus, the impact of planning can be seen in more than one section of PPB documents.

To provide guidance to the people in the Coast Guard who prepare the various PPB submissions, the Coast Guard uses its long-range view to state broad objectives and policies. This is divided into three sections: objectives, policies, and projections. Two objectives are: to minimize loss of life, personal injury and property damage on, over and under the high seas and water subject to United States jurisdiction; and to facilitate waterborne activity in support of national economic, scientific, defense, and social needs. The discussion of Coast Guard policy points out: "The Coast Guard will provide services and effective systems to facilitate marine transportation. Service will include but not be limited to provisions of information, coordination, and advice. Systems contribute to the efficient movement of vessels both at sea and in congested or port areas." The projections section of the long-range view points out: "The possibility of vessel-to-vessel and vessel-to-structure collisions will increase as larger, deeper draft vessels move into operation and as the number of offshore structures proliferate." It proceeds: "There will also be a greater possibility of surface and submersible vessel collisions."[40]

The first step in PPB is establishing an accepted long-range plan, which, in turn, is based upon planning proposals. One such planning proposal, the audio-visual (or short-range) aids proposal based upon the Booz Allen work, is discussed earlier in this chapter. The plan was completed and accepted by the chief of staff. It contained such policy positions as: to replace existing steel buoys with plastic buoys where feasible and to extend the intervals between routine servicing visits for all aids. The plan itself is quite long and detailed. The summary contains nine single-spaced pages.[41]

The next step is the plan summary. The program manager submitted a plan summary to the chief of staff. The summary contained specific assumptions being made, the basis for making the assumptions, specific goals it hoped to achieve, and implementation steps. This summary served as a guide for later budget action. Some difficulty was experienced in meeting the format requirements, especially on such matters as distinguishing between "milestones" and "implementation steps."[42] The following illustrates the major features of the document and shows how it ties together the long-range view, plans, and later program decisions.[43]

A. *OBJECTIVE*—To minimize loss of life, personal injury and property damage on, over and under the high seas and waters subject to United States jurisdiction.

1. *Goal I. Provide All Weather Navigation Capability, Responsive to User Needs. . . .*
2. *Goal II. Provide an Effective Audio/Visual Aids to Navigation Systems Responsive to User Needs*
   a. ASSUMPTIONS
      (1) Facts. . . .
         (c) Fixed structures are more effective aids to the mariner than buoys and are less costly to maintain. Approximately 20% of existing buoys can be replaced with fixed structures, based on the Geonautics and Booz-Allen Study. . . .
   Milestone II. Reduce the Cost of Operating and Maintaining the Audio/ Visual Aids to Navigations Subsystem While Maintaining or Improving the Present Level of Effectiveness
      (1) *Implementation Steps. . . .*
         (b) Continue replacement and decommissioning of appropriate lightships. Replace 3 lightships with large navigation buoys.

Program determinations represent the total Coast Guard "agreement" on the problems and goals that merit major emphasis in the forthcoming budget year.[44] The determination avoids discussion of alternative solutions but lays the ground for the major decision-making step of writing and ranking resource change proposals (RCP). Some of the problems identified in the program determination as warranting budgetary emphasis were: "We do not have enough trained and experienced aid to navigation servicing personnel," and "Most A to N vessels are overaged and have substandard habitability."[45] Some milestones that warranted budget emphasis were: complete major renovation of two C or B class WLBs (servicing vessels); accomplish austere renovation of five WLBs; complete design of inshore buoy tenders; complete 20 percent of the program to replace buoys with aids on fixed structures; and complete the evaluation of lighted plastic buoys to replace steel buoys.[46]

Resource change proposals are the documents used by program managers to request a change in resource required in a program. The chief of staff's Programs Division reviews these documents, comments on them, allows the program managers to improve their RCPs, and ranks them. These recommendations are then reviewed and appeals heard by a Coordination Board composed of the deputy program managers. Priorities are established by the board. The program proposal is addressed to the changes that can be funded within the "budget limit" established by the department and OMB. The chief of staff's Plans Evaluation Division uses the RCPs as a basis for determining their consonance with long-range plans, and if they do not match, revisions are required. The Budget Division uses the RCP as basic input for the annual budget documents.[47]

RCP No. 75 was developed for Fiscal Year 1973, and it illustrates how the Coast Guard places a priority on the three hundred-plus RCPs each year. This RCP involves improving buoy tenders so that the life of 180-foot buoy tenders could be extended. Three alternative approaches to resolving the problem must be presented with the cost and implication of each alternative discussed. Samples of these presentations are shown in Appendix 5a. Figure 5A-1 (pp. 00-00) presents a sample of an RCP prepared and evaluated by the Programs Division. Each RCP is ranked. Figure 5A-2 (p. 00) is a copy of a "score card" used for RCP No. 75. Aids to navigation RCPs have consistently ranked very high. Figure 5A-3 (p. 00) is a copy of the first page of the FY 1974 priorities, which shows four aids to navigation RCPs. Each one directly evolved out of the earlier planning efforts.

The program proposal (or spring preview) is submitted annually to the department about May 1. This document specifies the programs and related resources required for the budget year. It is developed by the program managers specifically from the decisions made on the RCPs. The Programs Division reviews the draft program proposals and recommends adjustment. Eventually a draft is approved by the deputy chief of staff, and the draft proposals are returned to the program managers for preparation of the "smooth." The smooth program proposals for all subcategories are bound into one document by the Programs Division and submitted for approvals and transmitted to the department.[48]

The FY 1973 spring preview recommended two major policy changes involving aids to navigation: renovation of offshore buoy tenders, and national implementation plan for Loran C coverage; continental U.S. coastal/confluence area.

The spring preview pointed out that the present serving vessels for offshore marine navigation aids system were approaching thirty years of heavy operation and that something had to be done to improve the equipment and poor living conditions of the crews. This section summarized the information present in RCP 75 (Figure 5A-1) and recommended fourteen major renovations, twelve austere renovations, and twelve new constructions. A total of $1,200,000 was needed in FY 1973, but thirty-four fewer Coast Guard positions were required.[49] This was approved by the department, OMB, and Congress.[50]

The more controversial Loran C radio navigation proposal was also made in the FY 1973 spring preview. The document pointed out that Loran C coverage was inadequate "to provide an electronic navigation system that meets the needs of the U.S. Maritime interests in the regions of the high seas; coastal confluence; and harbor, estuary and Marine terminals." This recommendation was a direct result of the National Plan for Navigation Effort and PPB analyses as explained earlier. The spring preview recommended the Loran C radio navigation system and requested $2,837,000 in FY 1973 funds to implement that policy decision.[51] This was not approved by the department, and as discussed previously in this chapter, more analysis was requested. In FY 1974, the policy question was again put to the department via the spring preview.[52]

A very obvious conclusion can be reached from the above discussion: PPB was used as an integral aspect of policy decision-making in the Coast Guard.

Conclusions

One must be careful to point out the rather limited scope of this chapter. Most of the policy questions involved highly technical considerations that lend themselves to the more rational analysis associated with PPB. Some political overtones were present, but they were not nearly as dominant as they were in connection with events noted in the two previous chapters. This chapter does illustrate that while policy analysis is an integral part, it is not always the dominant aspect, of government decision-making.

Appendix 5A:
Coast Guard Working Papers

DEPARTMENT OF TRANSPORTATION U.S. COAST GUARD CGHQ-4302A (Rev. 11-70)	RESOURCE CHANGE PROPOSAL PART I – SUMMARY	1. PROGRAM AN		
		2. RCP NO. 75C	3. ID 1-8	4. BY 197<u>3</u>

5. RCP TITLE   Improve Buoy Tenders

6. PURPOSE   Extend the life of 180' Tenders

APPROXIMATION OF NET RESOURCE CHANGES REQUIRED	BUDGET YEAR ($000's)			5-YR ($000's)		
	TOTAL COST	TOTAL PERS.		TOTAL COST	TOTAL PERS.	
		MIL	CIV		MIL	CIV
7. ALTERNATIVE A Major renovation 14 WLB's (2 FY 73) Austere Renovation 12 WLB's – (0 FY 73)	1,158	(−78)	0	13,069	(−498)	0
8. ALTERNATIVE B Major renovation 26 WLB's (2 FY 73)	875	(−78)	0	19,230	(−1,122)	0
9. ALTERNATIVE C Construct new class of offshore tender (0 FY 73) Austere renovation 19 WLB's (4 FY 73)	434	0	0	26,866	37	0
10. ALTERNATIVE D						

11. IF APPROVED, WILL THIS CONSTITUTE MOVING INTO A NEW OR DISTINCTIVE FIELD OF ENDEAVOUR FOR THE COAST GUARD?   ☐ YES   ☒ NO

IF YES, WHAT IS THE AUTHORITY OR MANDATE FOR IT?

IF THE AUTHORITY OR MANDATE IS NON-STATUTORY ATTACH DOCUMENTATION.

DOCUMENTATION ATTACHED?   ☐ YES   ☒ NO

12. IS LEGISLATION REQUIRED   ☐ YES   ☒ NO

13. IS AN ENVIRONMENTAL IMPACT STATEMENT REQUIRED?   ☐ YES   ☒ NO   ☐ DONE

14. THE FOLLOWING SUPPORT MANAGERS HAVE BEEN CONSULTED IN PREPARING THIS RCP
☐ GAP   ☐ GAF   ☐ GAC   ☐ GAS   ☐ R&D
GA SPECIFY   ☐ LEGAL   ☐ IG   ☐ MEDICAL   OTHERS

15. RCP PREPARED BY	16. TEL. NO.	17. DATE PREPARED 7/22/71	18. PROGRAM/SUPPORT MANAGER SIGNATURE
19. PROGRAM SUPPORT DIRECTOR SIGNATURE			20. DATE APPROVED

PREVIOUS EDITIONS ARE OBSOLETE   Marine Environment and Systems   PAGE 1

DEPARTMENT OF TRANSPORTATION U.S. COAST GUARD CGHQ-4302C (Rev. 11-70)	RESOURCE CHANGE PROPOSAL PART I – ANALYSIS	1. PROGRAM AN		
		2. RCP NO. 75C	3. ID 1-8	4. BY 197<u>3</u>

5. RCP TITLE
Improve Buoy Tenders

6. THIS RCP IF INTENDED TO ☒ SOLVE A PROBLEM ☐ REACH A GOAL ENROUTE TO ONE OF OUR LONG RANGE OBJECTIVES

7. NARRATIVE DESCRIPTION OF PROBLEM OR GOAL (Complete here. Use short paragraphs)

The entire WLB fleet is approaching 30 years of age. Timely replacement and/or renovation action must be taken if the Coast Guard is to avoid the problems concomitant to operating an average fleet with substandard habitability conditions.

PROGRAM DETERMINATIONS FY 73: "Most buoy tenders are experiencing high maintenance costs and have substandard habitability. The life of selected tenders can be extended into the 1980's by extensive rehabilitation."

8. LIST OF GOVERNING STANDARDS OR CRITERIA (Quantitative)

The habitability of WLB's is far below the standards of recent Coast Guard construction such as 378' WHEC's, 210' WHEC's, or 157' WLM's.

9. BACKGROUND (Complete here. Use short paragraphs)

The Booz-Allen Study of the Short Range Aids servicing system has prompted adoption/investigation of several concepts which, if successful and adequately funded, could reduce AN requirements for 180' WLB's from the present 37 to approximately 26 by 1977. These concepts concern: adoption of plastic buoys, replacement of buoys with structures, Aids to Navigation Teams (ANTs), and revised servicing schedules and discrepancy response criteria.

A modest OE funded program to overhaul main propulsion systems was begun in FY 69. In the FY 72 budget funds have been requested to begin a limited habitability improvement program. This RCP requests a shift of funding from OE to A,C,I and requests additional A,C,I funds for a large scale renovation program which will entail major renovations of 14 WLB's requiring an icebreaking capability and "austere" renovation of 12 others which will operate until replaced by new construction in the period 1978-82.

Those WLB's which undergo major renovation will satisfy AN operational requirements for an Offshore Tender with icebreaking capability for the next 15-20 years when a replacement program for those vessels will begin.

PREVIOUS EDITIONS ARE OBSOLETE   PAGE 2

DEPARTMENT OF TRANSPORTATION U.S. COAST GUARD CGHQ-4302D (11-70)	RESOURCE CHANGE PROPOSAL PART I — ANALYSIS (Cont'd)	1. PROGRAM AN		
		2. RCP NO. 75C	3. ID 1-8	4. BY 1973

5. RCP TITLE
Improve Buoy Tenders

Below and on the next 3 sheets analyze 4 alternative courses of action that would in whole or partially, solve the problem or attain the goal. The "don't do it" alternative is presumed as a fifth choice, so do not include it. Discuss the alternatives in the order of priority. Use only the space provided. Do not extend to extra pages.

6. ALTERNATIVE (A) (Preferred Alternative)

7. DESCRIPTION
Major renovation of 14 WLB's and austere renovation of 12 WLB's beginning with FY 73 major renovation of 2 WLB C/B class tenders at a cost of $1,364,000 each. This renovation will consist of: extensive habitability improvements, main propulsion system overhaul, installation of 100 KW generators, air conditioning, new engines, improved cargo handling equipment, installation of a bow thruster, and extensive structural preservation.

8. APPROXIMATION OF NET RESOURCE CHANGES REQUIRED ($000's)

	BY	BY + 1	BY + 2	BY + 3	BY + 4
AC&I	2,728	7,247	7,711	5,862	0
R&D/BA					
OE/RT (−OR−) OR NON-R	−(1,570)	−(2,096)	−(2,227)	−(2,804)	−(1,782)
PERS. CHANGES—END OF YR. + OFF. + WO + ENL. + CIV.	-9-2-67-0	-9-2-80-0	-14-3-120-0	-14-3-133-0	-0-0-42-0

9. BENEFITS EXPECTED (Include Outputs where appropriate)
QUANTITATIVE (Equate to stds. & criteria where possible)
This program, in conjunction with the planned replacement of those WLB's not requiring an icebreaking capability, will provide the Coast Guard with an offshore tender fleet which will meet AN operational requirements for the next 15-30 years, while maintaining a relatively stable level of ACI expenditures. The rotational vessel concept will allow the accomplishment of this renovation with a minimum of hardship to personnel and minimum disruption to operating schedules.

Greatly improve habitability on all WLB's by the end of FY 77.

OTHER
Allow time to develop new buoys, handling techniques, and to assess the impact of related programs (see C-2-9) on replacement vessel design. Avoid block vessel replacement programs in the future.

10. IMPACT ON CG PEOPLE
WORKLOAD
Increase workload on units in districts from which rotational vessels are drawn. This increased workload should be easily absorbed after implementation, presently underway, of new servicing schedules and discrepancy response criteria and implementation of new servicing concepts such as ANTs.

Living Conditions (incl. Safety) — Greatly improve.

Working Conditions — Enhance reliability, maneuverability, and safety, as well as crew comfort.

11. IMPACT ON SUPPORTING ACTIVITIES AND OTHER PROGRAMS
R&D None
TRAINING
Some training of crews in the operation and maintenance of new equipment.
ENG. & MAINTENANCE
New engines and other equipment will require less maintenance and provide greater reliability. Structural preservation will reduce hull and deck maintenance.
SUPPLY & CONTRACTING
Fewer overhauls and breakdowns should reduce the support required from Supply. Anticipated support problems for present engines will be avoided.
OTHER (Specify)

DEPARTMENT OF TRANSPORTATION U.S. COAST GUARD CGHQ-4302E (11-70)	RESOURCE CHANGE PROPOSAL PART I – ANALYSIS (Cont'd)	1. PROGRAM AN		
		2. RCP NO. 75C	3. ID 1-8	4. BY 1973

5. RCP TITLE
Improve Buoy Tenders

6. ALTERNATIVE (B)

7. DESCRIPTION
Perform major renovation on 26 WLB's beginning with 2 in FY 73. Major renovation to consist of: extensive habitability improvements, installation of 100 KW gneerators and air conditioning, new engines, improved cargo handling equipment, addition of a bow thruster, main propulsion system over haul, and structural preservation. Cost $1,364,000.
26 WLB's to have major renovation by 1977.

8. APPROXIMATION OF NET RESOURCE CHANGES REQUIRED ($000's)

	BY	BY +1	BY + 2	BY + 3	BY + 4
AC&I	2,728	10,184	8,148	8,184	6,184
R&D/BA					
OE/RT (−OR−) R OR NON-R	−(1,853)	−(2,993)	−(3,331)	−(3,912)	−(4,145)
PERS. CHANGES—END OF YR. + OFF. + WO + ENL. + CIV.	-9-2-67-0	-18-4-154-0	-18-4-174-0	-22-11-293-0	-22-11-313-0

9. BENEFITS EXPECTED (Include Outputs where appropriate)
QUANTITATIVE (Equate to stds. & criteria where possible)
This program will provide the Coast Guard with a WLB fleet which should adequately meet AN needs for an offshore tender for the next 15-20 years.

The need for a WLB replacement program will be postponed 15-20 years.

Greatly improve habitability on all WLB's by end of FY 78. Other allocations to develop new buoys, handling technques, and to assess the impact of related programs (see 0-2-9) on replacement vessel design.

10. IMPACT ON CG PEOPLE
WORKLOAD –
Increase workload on units in districts from which rotational vessels are taken. This increased workload should easily be absorbed after implementation of new servicing schedules, discrepancy response policies, and servicing concepts.

Living Conditions – Greatly improve.

WORKING CONDITIONS (Incl. Safety) – Enhance reliability, maneuverability, and
safety, as well as crew comfort.

11. IMPACT ON SUPPORTING ACTIVITIES AND OTHER PROGRAMS
R&D —

TRAINING – Same as Alt. A.

ENG. & MAINTENANCE – Same as Alt. A.

SUPPLY & CONTRACTING – Same as Alt. A.

OTHER (Specify) –

12. WHY IS THIS ALTERNATIVE NOT PREFERRED?
Is not the least cost alternative. Does not avoid the need for a block replacement program at a future date. Does not provide for a stable ACI expenditure level. Will not allow the early phase out of unneeded icebreaking hulls.

DEPARTMENT OF TRANSPORTATION U.S. COAST GUARD CGHQ-4302E (11-70)	RESOURCE CHANGE PROPOSAL PART I — ANALYSIS (Cont'd)	1. PROGRAM AN		
		2. RCP NO. 75C	3. ID 1-8	4. BY 197_3_

5. RCP TITLE Improve Buoy Tenders

6. ALTERNATIVE (C)

7. DESCRIPTION

Replace the present WLB fleet with new construction, prototype to be built FY 75. Estimated Cost: $ 8,200,000 per ship.

Perform austere renovation on 19 ships beginning with 4 FY 73 to ensure selected ships will perform adequately and improve habitability until replaced in approximately 10 years. This renovation will consist of: extensive habitability improvements, propulsion system overhaul, addition of 100 KW generators and air conditioning. Cost approximately $ 371,000 each.

8. APPROXIMATION OF NET RESOURCE CHANGES REQUIRED ($000's)

	BY	BY + 1	BY + 2	BY + 3	BY + 4
AC&I	1,484	1,855	10,426	1,484	16,400
R&D/BA					
OE/RT (−OR−) R OR NON-R	−(1,050)	−(1,050)	−(1,050)	−(536)	−(1,097)
PERS. CHANGES—END OF YR. + OFF. + WO + ENL. + CIV.	0	0	0	+4+2+37+0	-0-0-6-0

9. BENEFITS EXPECTED (Include Outputs where appropriate)
Quantitative (Equate to stds. & criteria where possible) —

This program will provide a modern offshore tender fleet of all new vessels by 1986.

OTHER

10. IMPACT ON CG PEOPLE

WORKLOAD — None

LIVING CONDITIONS — Greatly improve.

WORKING CONDITIONS (Incl. Safety) — Enhance reliability, safety, and crew comfort.

11. IMPACT ON SUPPORTING ACTIVITIES AND OTHER PROGRAMS

R&D — None

TRAINING — Same as Alts. A & B.

ENG. & MAINTENANCE — Same as Alts. A & B.

SUPPLY & CONTRACTING — Same as Alts. A & B.

OTHER (Specify) —

12. WHY IS THIS ALTERNATIVE NOT PREFERRED?

This is the most costly alterative. Vessel hulls with years of useful life remaining will be replaced. Does not avoid the need for a block replacement program at a future date. Does not allow time to develop new buoys, handling techniques, or to assess the impact of related programs (see C-2-9) on replacement vessel design.

RCP #   75   ID   1   APPN   OG

Program   A4

Item	Score
1. Impact on available resources	7
2. Mandate	7
3. Documentation	9
4. Public benefit	1
5. Effect on personnel workload	5
6. Effect on living conditions	9
7. Impact on plant	7
8. Impact on Training	7
9. Support Managers prepared	7

TOTAL | 1112 |

10. PM/PD priority   9

Figure 5A-2. Sample "Score Card."

65

C505RMR5
05/10/72

BUDGET DEVELOPMENT SYSTEM
OE BUDGET CHANGES + PRIORITIES FY 1974, FORECAST STAGE

PAGE 1

PRIORITY RCP (1)(2)(4)(7)(9)	Q PROGRAM	ITEM DESCRIPTION	BILLETS AND POSITIONS				PERSONNEL ($000)	OTHER ($000) (19)	BUD (24)	REIM (27)
			OFFICERS (10)	WARRANTS (12)	ENLISTED (14)	CIVILIAN (17)				
A		CHANGES (MANDATORY)								
A 1 678.01	GA	Terminations and Reductions						3,472—		
A 2 677.01	GA	Annualization						3,811		
A 3 75.01E2	AN	WLB Renovation	5—	3—	49—		336—	50—		
A 4 97.01C 2	AN	Lamp			48—		214—			
A 5 47.01C 2	GAP	Fam Hsg Const/Furn/Support Personnel			9	3		200—		
A 6 809.01	GAP	Command at Sea Pay						110		
A 7 689.02C 2	GAP	New Enlisted Uniforms				15	77	3,137		
A 8 805.01	GA	Sh 30 General Col Increases						5,873		
A 8 805.02	GA	Sh 30 Most Nation Loran						557		
A 8 805.03	GA	Sh 30 WB Pay Increases						1,483		
A 9 207.01C 2	AN	Base Portsmouth Phase II						189		
A 10 658.01A 2	MEP	Environmental Impact Statement Staff	16			12	214			
A 11 46.20C 2	GAP	Care may Follow on Operating Expense						5		
A 12 104.01C 2	AN	Waterways Aton Follow On OE						180		
A 13 375.03	MEP	CG Shore Station Pollution Abatement						500		
A 14 375.02	MEP	Abate Paint Spray Facility Air Poll						127		

Figure 5A-3. Sample Page, FY 1974 Priorities.

6

Policy Analysis and Public Policymaking

What can reasonably be expected of policy analysis as it relates to public policymaking? Two points might be made in summary: first, PPB was an attempt in the Johnson administration to apply and use systematically one approach to governmental policy decisions, including resource allocations. The formal characteristics of PPB were the program memorandum (PM), special analytical studies, program and financial plans, program structure, and program issues. As Chapter 2 illustrated, departments and agencies emulated or built upon some of the PPB characteristics. For example, UMTA created UMTA studies that corresponded to the special analytical studies. The U.S. Coast Guard Resource Change Proposal served as an essential input into the departmental PM called the program proposal. With the exception of the Coast Guard, however, the formal characteristics of PPB were largely ignored by the department and its agencies. Decisions, of course, were made, but PPB's formal mechanisms were seldom used as decision-making aids. Still, PPB did significantly affect *some* decisions, particularly those associated with special studies.

A second point is that PPB should not be equated to policy analysis. This is most important. PPB was intended to be one decision-making system; it was an attempt to systematically incorporate policy analysis into public policymaking. The distinction between the PPB and policy analysis is explained in Chapter 1. PPB (or PPBS) is officially dead in the federal government, but policy analysis is alive. A former Nixon deputy director of OMB, Fred Malick, has publicly said that analytical concepts and techniques associated with PPB will continue to be important and that OMB will place strong emphasis on program evaluation and analysis.[1]

One very knowledgeable former assistant director of OMB, who helped introduce PPB into the Johnson administration, claimed at that time that "systematic analysis in government" would affect policy decisions and that some decisions would be better. The previous chapters tend to substantiate his claim that "*some* decisions will be different from what they otherwise would be without this approach." This book does not and cannot substantiate his claim that "some of these decisions will be better than they would have been absent the use of more formalized analysis." As he himself points out: "The last statement can only, in the final analysis, be defended as an individual value judgment and cannot in any meaningful sense be substantiated."[2]

The Underappreciated Factors

In the literature on PPB, occasional cases may be found in which the political, human, and operational factors are discussed as determining the success of PPB in one or another federal department or agency. (Alain C. Enthoven, Charles L. Schultz and Charles J. Hitch, in particular, noted the significance of these factors.)[3] The emphasis in the literature, however, is upon more analytical matters, those involving the technical application of PPB. It is a contention of this study that the significance of the political, human, and operational factors in successfully applying systematic analysis to the formulation of public policy was not appreciated or, at least, was not emphasized enough.

PPB operated within the context of the political process. Greater reliance on more formal analysis of policy issues and alternatives did not produce change in the underlying decision-making structure of the American system of government.[4] Several authors (Wildavsky, Fenno, and Woll) have described this underlying process, the relationships and roles that explain the traditional policymaking factors influencing an agency's decision-makers.[5] The previous chapters illustrate and confirm the commonly accepted conclusion that outside groups do influence agency policy. One can diagrammatically represent some of the influencing groups as shown in Figure 6-1.

Thus, at least three groups directly influence an agency: (1) the Executive Office of the President, (2) the Congress, and (3) clientele groups. For example, in the instance of project selection criteria for the urban transportation capital grant program (Chapter 4), the OMB (a part of the Executive Office) used the approach of requiring a special analytical study to force the UMTA to change its policy on how it selected projects for funding. The discussion on the New Systems Study in Chapter 3 illustrates how a single congressman can influence an agency to undertake a massive rethinking on the direction of its research and development effort. Finally, the discussion in Chapter 4 on the urban mass transportation operating subsidy and capital grant criteria illustrates how a clientele group influences Congress and an agency. Fred Burke, a professional

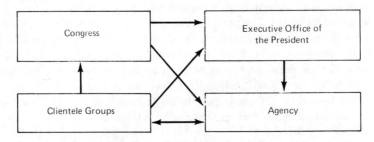

Figure 6-1. Influence Relationships

lobbyist, did influence the shaping of legislation and did work with and influence UMTA in its revision of its project selection criteria.

The mood of the country toward an agency's program is a political factor and a very significant one.[6] Aware of this, the transit lobby gave the impression to Congress that very few influencing groups in the country were against the transit legislation and, in fact, that many key groups were strongly in favor of the legislation. The belief that strong popular support exists creates a positive image or favorable attitude toward an agency's legislation, which in turn affects policy analysis and decision-making. For example, in the FY 1974 spring preview submission, UMTA did not request added funding for its capital grant program. The effect of a positive popular attitude toward a program was dramatically illustrated when Undersecretary Beggs suggested to UMTA that they might wish to reconsider and request additional funding for that program. This was at a time when other programs were being cut back.

An agency can cultivate an advantageous political environment by cooperating with its clientele groups.[7] The transit lobby obviously influences Congress. If UMTA wished to expand the capital grant program or create a new operating subsidy program, thus enlarging its "empire," then cooperation with the transit lobby would put added pressure on the Executive Office to change its policy toward transit. Ironically, in the case of UMTA, the agency was negative toward new programs and a close working relationship with the clientele groups did not exist, although a closer relationship was being established as this book was being written.

Strong and effective political resistance to PPB existed in the bureaucracy. This was sometimes manifested in an agency alliance with its respective constituency groups and key congressmen and senators. As pointed out in Chapter 2, the Federal Highway Administration was able to resist the implementation of PPB. It had its own decision-making process (which did use analysis) and did not wish to adopt the PPB approach. The Federal Highway Administration has enjoyed a strong constituency group and supportive key congressmen and senators. Under such circumstances, the likelihood of the department being able to force FHWA compliance on this largely procedural issue was highly unlikely.

The human factor is a particularly neglected subject in the literature on program budgeting and policy analysis. The literature stresses that the agency head must support program analysis if that activity is to have any significance in agency decision-making.[8] The decision on the Urban Tracked Air Cushion Vehicle (TACV) demonstration (Chapter 3) illustrates the obvious fact that a secretary can override any decision and decide himself whether a specific project will be undertaken. The chapter on aids to navigation, however, illustrates that an agency head can take seriously a procedural formality such as systematic policy analysis and use it in deciding agency policy.

The significance of a key employee resisting a change should also be noted.[9]

In the FY 1974 spring preview departmental review, Undersecretary Beggs stressed the importance of the new project selection criteria and how they must be implemented. However, the assistant administrator for program operations, William Hurd, had refused to let Bob McManus brief Hurd's staff on the new project selection criteria that the Office of Program Operations was charged with implementing. Bill Hurd thought the criteria were ridiculous. The author vividly recalls Hurd's strong emotions and his dramatic decision to retire. The Program Operations staff had a strong bias against the new criteria and yet were supposed to make it operational in less than two weeks. Obviously, the resistance of a key person in an agency can be a significant factor in actual policy implementation.

The human element in policy analysis and decision-making can be significant in other ways. If a policy analyst assigned to a project produces a report that does not offer a positive or politically practical recommendation, his report can become a target of criticism for this failure to offer a solution that politicians can act upon. The data and findings of a valuable study can be completely ignored in such a case. For example, the transit lobby group and Congress did not like the DOT policy analysts' report on transit operating subsidies. The policy analysts had questioned the effectiveness of operating subsidies and could not recommend them. The report was severely criticized by the transit lobby and Congress for its lack of a positive suggestion. On these grounds, lobbyist William J. Ronan, president of the Institute for Rail Transit, appealed to the secretary to change the report. The secretary responded to the criticism with a request to UMTA that a specific operating subsidy proposal be developed.

The literature on PPB also points out that the people in the agency must believe that the PPB process has significance and legitimacy.[10] Such a feeling did not exist in UMTA regarding the research and development decisions. According to the DOT and UMTA orders, program decisions should have been reviewed by the program analysis group. In point of fact, decisions were often made directly by the secretary on very large projects such as TACV, the Morgantown people-mover, and the Transpo 72 people-mover demonstrations.

Regardless of the ultimate wisdom of these one-man decisions, this approach to decision-making did not reinforce the significance and legitimacy of PPB. The author can recall a two-week period during the preparation of a spring preview when it was necessary to redraft completely the R and D justification three times because the secretary and Congress were reprogramming current-year R and D projects. The PPB documents were used not for decision-making but merely to meet a requirement. Systematic policy analysis was impossible, because important overriding political factors were directly involved. It was not surprising that the information received from the Office of Research and Development was merely descriptive and did not permit analysis.

The above situations are a marked contrast to events and procedures in the Coast Guard aids to navigation program. Interviewed Coast Guard officers stressed that PPB was a reality in the Coast Guard and one had to follow the system if a policy change was to occur. Political factors were sometimes important, but internally the rules of the game for making policy change were in the PPB manual.[11]

The literature of PPB mentions that key groups in an agency must not feel hostile to the change.[12] In getting the aids to navigation changes accepted in the agency, much effort was devoted to selling the changes to the various internal groups within the Coast Guard. The apparent acceptance by Coast Guard personnel tends to support the hypothesis that internal selling and consultation efforts in an agency, particularly in the planning stage, reduces internal resistance and increases the likelihood of successful implementation of the change.

The presence or absence of cooperative working relations is another important factor in the effective use of PPB.[13] These relationships are critical if there is to be a linking of planning, policy analysis, and budgeting.[14] (The budget unit often proves particularly difficult to integrate into the system.) The previous chapters indicate that cooperative working relationships in UMTA and the Coast Guard did exist, and that they were particularly cooperative, and therefore particularly effective, in the Coast Guard. The Coast Guard example illustrates that planning, policy analysis, and budgeting can be effectively linked.

A few more rather obvious operational factors are essential in order to have successful policy analysis in an agency. There must be a sufficient number of talented people to carry out the policy analysis activity. There should be sufficient data and an adequate information system available to the analyst. There must be sufficient funding to support the activity. There should be a sufficient number of outside experts or consultants to support the program analyst.[15] Consultants serve as an added resource of talent and are often used for gathering information, but use of their services is obviously predicated on the availability of funds to hire them as well as the willingness of government officials to use them. If consultants are used, there should be a capable in-house analyst who can take the consultant's work, review it properly, and mold the product to fit the agency's needs. A good use of consultants is illustrated in the discussion on aids to navigation.

Any successful implementation of systematic analysis in government must take into account the above political, human, and operational factors. In many instances, as illustrated in the previous three chapters, those attempting to implement PPB failed, not because of poor techniques, but because of the negative influence of one or more of those factors. A careful examination of the early literature on PPB reveals that the significance of those factors was understood, but stress was placed upon discussing more analytically oriented topics. It is therefore not surprising that neither the Johnson nor the Nixon administrations systematically confronted these factors in a conscious attempt to better facilitate the implementation of PPB. In fairness to the Johnson administration, it should be pointed out that a training effort was undertaken.

This, however, did not constitute a systematic attempt to meet directly the problems presented by the factors discussed here.

Weaknesses of PPB

As a major administration innovation, PPB became quite topical; there was much discussion of the weaknesses of PPB. Some of the weaknesses mentioned related to the political, human, and operational factors discussed in the previous section. Some critics attacked as false the conceptual assumptions underlying PPB. In some instances, the "weaknesses" cited belied a concern about centralization of government or the effect of PPB on reorganizations. The case examples of decision-making presented in the previous three chapters can serve as a basis for discussing some of the "weaknesses." In order to facilitate discussion, the "weaknesses" are grouped into four sets of difficulties in the design of the PPB system: conceptual, political, managerial, and implementation.

Commonly cited conceptual difficulties underlying PPB were: (1) program budgeting is too vague a concept to be made meaningfully operational; (2) the use of a program structure makes analysis much more difficult, if not impossible; (3) it is impossible to reach any kind of reasonable consensus on broad objectives; and (4) analysis is useful only for more narrow policy questions.[16]

Critics of PPB said "Program budgeting cannot be stated in operational terms. There is no agreement on what the words mean, let alone an ability to show another person what should be done. The reason for the difficulty is that telling an agency to adopt program budgeting means telling it to find better policies and there is no formula for doing that."[17] The wide variety of approaches to PPB, as documented in Chapter 2, tends to confirm the ambiguities of the program budgeting concept. In spite of the ambiguities of the program budgeting concept, Chapter 5 illustrates that the concept can be implemented. Thus, any strong statement saying otherwise is improper. This conclusion must be qualified to point out that the aids to navigation program deals with more technical and less politically sensitive issues. Under different circumstances, the ambiguities may contribute to preventing the successful implementation of program budgeting.

The use of a program structure was said to require a complete list of organizational objectives and to necessitate information that "led to a sham that piles up meaningless data under vague categories." The program structure characteristic of PPB hid rather than clarified issues, and it suggested comparisons among categories for which there was no factual or analytical basis.[18] In Chapter 2 it was pointed out that a program structure was a characteristic of PPB. In Chapters 3, 4, and 5, no case example involved the use of the program structure as a part of an analysis or part of decision-making. Where analysis was used, other analytical considerations were employed. This omission of the program structure in analyses tends to confirm the belief that use of a program structure is not needed for analysis. Most policy decisions involving major projects or major program changes in DOT did not *involve* judging one program against another in the context of the program structure. Most policy issues revolved around some policy change limited exclusively to one program. This meant that the program structure was an inappropriate basis for analysis.

The third and fourth conceptual difficulties can be considered together. Critics point out that it is extremely difficult to get consensus on goals within a single area of policy. As a result, the policy analyst's attempts to find objectives may start at the highest levels of generalization, searching, for example, for a national consensus on what needs to be done. But finding a national consensus is normally so difficult that the analyst drops the level of generalization down to something that is more easily and readily accepted as an objective. For example, in education the analyst moves from general statements of what schools should be, down to such things as scholastic achievement, percentage of children going to college, and so on.[19] Chapter 2 points out that broad general objectives for the agencies were established in DOT. The discussion about project selection criteria in Chapter 4, however, illustrates how extremely difficult it is to frame acceptable broad objectives and how more operational objectives, such as ridership, are used to reinterpret the broader objective. Although it is often difficult to decide on high-level objectives, it can be done in many circumstances as long as one appreciates that: a given activity can meet several objectives, the objectives can be in conflict (e.g., a safety objective may override an efficiency objective), and the measures used to determine successful fulfillment of objectives are often unavoidably subject to methodological question.

Commonly cited difficulties concerned with the implementation of PPB were that: it was poorly introduced into government, those implementing it incorrectly assumed that all top management people (e.g., agency heads) would adopt PPB, and the Budget Bureau incorrectly assumed that program analysis would penetrate the budgetary process.[20] The discussion in the previous four chapters was not addressed directly to these points, but the facts presented do not conflict with these conclusions. In the Department of Transportation PPB existed, appropriate orders were drafted, and program planning units were established. No systematic talent search, training programs, or phased implementation plan was instituted. In other words, little preparation went into introducing PPB into the Department of Transportation, but a mandate did exist to implement it.

Those that established PPB were aware that "without the wholehearted understanding and support of the Cabinet and independent agency heads, . . . the effects of PPB would be marginal."[21] President Johnson said: "I have, therefore, asked the Budget Director to sit down with each of you to review your planning-programming-budgeting systems and give you his objective analysis of its effectiveness. He will then report to me on a quarterly basis . . . on the progress of your implementation of my directive."[22] In spite of this intention, there was no evidence in the Department of Transportation that a strong continuing effort was made to implement PPB. In fact, there was every indication that PPB was not particularly important. For example, at its peak, the Bureau of the Budget staff charged with monitoring and promoting the government-wide effort numbered fewer than a dozen professionals.[23] One can conclude that the Budget Bureau itself was not committed to PPB. Once the various departments and agencies tried PPB and subsequently discovered the Budget Bureau's apparent lack of commitment, it is not surprising that top department and agency management also soon lacked commitment.

One commentator on the death of PPB stressed that in a PPB system the fate of analysis hinged on its use in budgeting.

For all its preaching about an integrated planning and budgeting system, the Budget Bureau steadfastly kept the two apart, quarantining its tiny PPB operation from the powerful examinations and budget review staffs, and promulgating separate PPB and budget instructions. The departments could not accomplish for themselves what the Budget Bureau refused (or was unable) to do for itself.[24]

In UMTA and the Coast Guard, there was no problem in having policy decisions, arrived at in the context of policy analysis, reflected completely in the budget documents for the respective agencies. Planning and programming may have been poorly coordinated in the Budget Bureau, but that was not necessarily the situation in the departments. Possibly the limited successes of PPB in UMTA and the successes of the Coast Guard can be partly attributed to the relatively good relationship between program planning and the budget units. Of course, other factors such as its use by the agency head were significant. The previous chapters cannot confirm the significance of the "integrated" planning and budgeting activities.

There are five commonly cited political "difficulties" associated with PPB: (1) PPB disturbed the executive branch relationship to Congress by strengthening the executive branch; (2) PPB did not permit deliberately obscure objectives, which are sometimes politically advantageous; (3) PPB was antithetical to our political process; (4) the use of a five-year financial plan limited the political options available; and (5) analyses, associated with PPB, ignored highly important political costs and benefits.[25]

No evidence exists in the previous chapters that the use of PPB disturbed the traditional relationship of Congress to the executive branch, although some commentators reasoned that PPB would significantly strengthen the executive branch to the detriment of Congress. The PPB products were designed to improve the presidential budget decision process,[26] but PPB did not play a strong role in the public policymaking process in DOT. Congress did not alter its methods of operation. Congress did call for a study on transit operating subsidy that appeared very similar to a PPB special analytical study, but there was no evidence that this was prompted at all by PPB. The fear of the commentators appeared to be groundless if the case examples cited were typical in the federal government.

Some critics of PPB point out that some instances exist in which it is possible to reach agreement on certain programs even though the various political groups involved have conflicting or even antithetical values. They conclude that identifying objectives in an analysis would make agreement on programs and budgets that much more difficult.[27] The material in the previous chapters does not support this hypothesis, but a much more comprehensive research would be needed to investigate properly this hypothesis. It seems possible that such a set of circumstances could exist and that PPB or some other application of analysis would prevent a political agreement. However, in most political bargaining sessions the actors are conscious of the conflicting values present. A case can be made that analysis might help to convince opposing parties that a mutually accommodating solution was possible in spite of the conflicting values. Thus, it would seem that analysis could be either an aid or detriment to political bargaining depending on the circumstances involved.

All the above notwithstanding, a school of thought maintains that systematic analysis is such a superior approach to public policymaking that the existing political process should be radically altered.[28] Some systems analysts have been argued seriously that a third chamber of Congress composed of systems analysts be established as lawmakers. They justified this proposal with reasoning similar to that of an elitist political theorist.[29] Nothing said at DOT would in any way confirm this type of thinking. The advocates of PPB consider the system as complementary to the budgetary and program decision-making process.[30] It was intended to affect the policymaking and resource allocation process, but completely within the established political system.

Did the use of the five-year PPB plan limit the political options available to executive branch policymakers? The policy decisions in the previous chapters did not involve the program and financial plan. The passage of the UMTA 1970 legislation did, however, involve a five-year financial plan informally required by Congress. There was a great deal of trepidation about providing this to Congress, but once done, there was no apparent limiting of options, for Congress did not demand that the financial plan be followed. If Congress had demanded that the five-year financial plan be followed, this would have presented real difficulties. Congress rarely asks for documents such as the program and financial plan, which were considered internal documents within the executive branch. In some circumstances PFP might have limited the political options available, but such a phenomenon was not common if the DOT situation was typical.

The fifth underlying political difficulty cited was that analyses such as benefit-cost analysis, associated with PPB, ignored highly important political costs and benefits. The critics argue: "Designing a large-scale transportation system involves so close a mixture of political and economic considerations that it is not possible to disentangle them."[31] In the aids to navigation decision, the political factors were not the main analytical focus, but they were considered. For example, the fact that new equipment would have to be purchased by private operators (e.g., fishermen) forced the Coast Guard to consider the comparative cost of radio receivers. Political factors were also considered directly or indirectly in the UMTA policy studies. There was no political analysis of a proposal's impact upon a specific group of key congressmen or senators, but an astute reader could easily interpret the relative political costs and benefits in each of the major analyses discussed in Chapters 2 through 5. In the narrow meaning of the hypothesis, the difficulty can be said to be confirmed. In reality, however, it does not seem to be a problem.

The fourth set of difficulties attributed to PPB involves such topics as administrative centralization and reorganization. Did PPB lead to a significant increase in the centralization of the whole decision-making process? Did PPB, particularly owing to its "sensible program structure," foster significant reorganization?[32] A definite conclusion is impossible, for only a few decisions and programs are examined. The Office of Management and Budget did use PPB to exercise administrative control over UMTA's capital grant selection criteria. Also, the aids to navigation decision illustrates that analysis does facilitate a more centralized decision-making process. On the other hand, the urban transportation R and D policy was obviously directed by Secretary Volpe on several occasions without the benefit of PPB. There appears to be some basis to assert that PPB, when it works, does foster greater centralization of decision-making, but no firm conclusion is possible.

One commentator said: "I agree with the suggestion that, over time at least, reorganizations will be, if not compelled, at least strongly encouraged by the development of a sensible program structure."[33] The DOT experience cited does not confirm this forecast. Reorganizations occurred, but they did not apparently relate to PPB's program structure. Some reorganization in some parts of the federal government may have been encouraged by a program structure, but the facts cited in this book tend to dispute this generalization.

Limitations of Analysis

Analysis is generally agreed to be a "good" thing, but it does have limitations that should be considered when one decides to undertake policy analysis, especially comprehensive systematic efforts such as PPB. Some limitations of analysis are its high cost, the very poor data base that exists in this area, the difficulty in formulating goals and objectives, and the difficulty that policy-makers have in utilizing those analyses that are made. Also, policy analysis is an art form that requires intelligent analysts to make it work effectively. There are other limitations of analysis, but these are the most easily observed and commonly experienced ones.

Analysis is costly in terms of money, talent, and demand upon key employees' time. Analysis can vary significantly, but it does require highly trained and skilled individuals who commonly receive high salaries. The analysts, in turn, need expensive computers and require costly survey research and the collection of large amounts of information for their work. These already highly trained personnel require additional training to update their skills and so must attend professional conferences, formal training courses, and some additional university courses. If the work of these analysts is to be relevant to an organization, they must interact with program managers by seeking information and ideas. This interaction takes valuable time away from the people who must be concerned with the day-to-day operations of the organization. The analyst must, in many situations, even interact with the agency's leadership, whose time is usually limited at best.

Analysts normally must work with inadequate and poor information. Since information is expensive to acquire, most analysts must use information gathered for other purposes, such as trade information or census data. The information used normally is subject to serious methodological difficulties owing to (1) its unreliability, (2) its unavailability for use because of rights of privacy or long processing time, (3) improper sample size, (4) improper questionnaires, (5) poor frequency in collecting information, and (6) inadequate specificity. Added to this array of problems is the difficulty of manipulating the information in a timely manner so that serendipity is encouraged and information from various sources can be analyzed together.

An entirely different kind of limitation experienced with many forms of analysis is the formulation of goals and objectives. Analysis techniques often demand that a group's goals and objectives be clearly articulated. This often proves impossible, because ultimate values underlying objectives may vary significantly and individuals commonly have difficulty conceptualizing broad generalizations. Another factor is that activities commonly serve multiple purposes, and several conceptual and practical problems are created when one attempts to relate them to any given set of goals and objectives.

The fourth type of limitation—the difficulty policymakers have in utilizing analysis—has been discussed previously, but this limitation is so significant that it is discussed in more depth here. The ultimate user of analysis in a government agency is often a political appointee who will serve for an average of thirty months[34] and have no background in analysis.[35] During his tenure, he will experience a great demand on his time and have to bargain with other politically powerful persons for resources and favorable treatment in the process of reaching policy decisions. The analyses provided him will often be extremely difficult for a nonexpert to understand. He will also experience the common frustration of not having the analyses available to him at the optimum time for political bargaining purposes. Considering this environment, most agency heads will use analysis only when it is demanded by politically significant groups such as the Office of Management and Budget or the Congress. He may also use analysis if the person in charge of the analysis group is a strong, respected person. The general climate, however, discourages the use of analysis under normal circumstances.

Some attention should be given to benefit-cost analysis at this point, especially considering that this particular technique of analysis is the one most cited in texts.[36] Benefit-cost analysis is an evaluative technique that contrasts dollar value benefits with dollar value costs. It has been used extensively in justifying and evaluating public works projects sponsored by the Corps of Engineers, the Bureau of Reclamation, and the Federal Highway Administration. The method is to compute the project's benefits and cost and represent them as a ratio, with the underlying assumption that the good projects have a favorable ratio. Benefit-cost analysis was not used in any of the cases discussed in Chapters 3, 4, or 5, but the technique is used commonly in government.[37]

The technique has serious limitations. Only those benefits and costs that can be quantified are included directly in the analysis. In more sophisticated analysis, nonquantifiables are also mentioned, but the method prevents their being given equal treatment. In addition, the selection or exclusion of various benefits and costs as well as the dollar value assigned to them are subject to the analyst's preconceived biases. For example, an analyst can say that upgrading the transit service to poverty areas is a benefit and using some method he can assign a dollar amount to that benefit. However, the amount chosen by the analyst could be challenged. Also, another analyst could argue that such improved service is not a benefit.[38] The argument would then continue on a philosophic plane using concepts associated with Pareto and others.[39]

Other difficulties also exist. What is the *proper* discount rate?[40] How does one treat secondary and tertiary effects, such as the air pollution from automobiles on that new highway? Calculated benefits can often be challenged. For example, a new freeway exchange saved an extra one or two minutes for a commuter. What is the value, if anything, of that extra minute? Some would argue that one or two minutes saved on travel time cannot be considered a benefit because people do not think such units of time are valuable. The final benefit-cost ratio is normally open to dispute, as there is no established convention on how and what various costs and benefits should be computed.[41]

Benefit-cost analysis is ill-suited for many kinds of policy decisions. It does not appear to be useful for major project decisions such as the funding of a large water project or the decision to proceed with the supersonic transport (SST). These decisions are made through the political process. Benefit-cost does not appear to be well adapted to yes-or-no decisions, but it is more effective as a ranking tool. It is most useful for functions of government where efficiency is the paramount concern, and for decisions such as which maritime innovation should be pursued in order to increase shipping operating productivity. Benefit-cost analysis is less useful where great uncertainties exist, because unforeseen applications could conceivably make a significant difference in what should be recommended. Quantitative evaluation is particularly ill-suited for interprogram choices. For example, the choice between better health treatment or going to the moon is a value judgment best left to the voters or their representatives.[42]

One last point should be stressed; the cost of conducting benefit-cost analysis. The expenses of gathering the necessary data and hiring the necessary high-cost professional are very high. This must be weighed against the fact that the final benefit-cost analysis may not provide any more insight than a good man taking a few hours to think through the problem with another less complex analytical technique. The user of the analysis must judge whether benefit-cost analysis is "worth the cost."[43]

Considering the above, fair questions seem to be: "What is the reason for policy analysis? "What are the advantages?" Aaron Wildavsky defines policy analysis as the sustained application of intelligence and knowledge to social problems.[44] He points out that an investigation into any area reveals how little is known in that area compared to what is necessary to know in order to devise adequate policies. Also, in many agencies, no analytical test of program effectiveness has been developed. It is often not possible to determine whether the simplest objectives have been met. Wildavsky continues his explanation on the *raison d'etre* of policy analysis:

Policy analysis aims at providing information that contributes to making an agency politically and socially relevant. Policies are goals, objectives, and missions that guide the agency. Analysis evaluates and sifts alternative means and ends in the elusive pursuit of policy recommendations. By getting out of the firehouse environment of day-to-day administration, policy analysis seeks knowledge and opportunities for coping with an uncertain future. Because policy analysis is not concerned with projecting the *status quo*, but with tracing out the consequences of innovative ideas, it is a variant of planning. Complementing the agency's decision process, policy analysis is a tool of social change.[45]

In other words, the reason for policy analysis is dissatisfaction with present governmental decision-making approaches and a belief that the application of more intelligence and knowledge by the art form called policy analysis will result in better decisions.

Decision-Making

Decision-making, especially organizational decision-making, is a semistructured, indeed, largely informal procedure. The decision-making process includes much bargaining and coalition formation and exchanges of favors affected by power calculations and personal relations.[46] The nature of this process and the factors that influence it were illustrated in the previous chapters, particularly in the discussion of the decisions involving urban mass transportation research and development.

The decision-making models described in Chapter 1 can provide insight into the role of policy analysis in public policymaking. A model is an abstract representation of reality, or what we would prefer reality to be, which permits us to focus upon salient factors and ignore other factors not relevant to the subject matter under consideration. As a tool that enables us to understand and deal with complex phenomena, a model can be judged "good" or "bad" in terms of its usefulness in a given context. A hammer, for example, may be a "good" tool for building a shed, but it is "bad" for chopping wood. The same criterion of "being useful in a given context" applies equally well to the decision-making models described in Chapter 1. By first determining the correct criteria by which to judge these models, one can isolate the models useful for gaining the desired insights. Careful consideration of the implications of the "good" models then makes it possible to achieve better understanding of the real and potential role of policy analysis in public policymaking.

Selection of useful criteria for evaluating decision-making models must be guided by an understanding of why PPB was established. Part of the reason for creating PPB was a belief that governmental decision-making should be improved and that important public policy decisions were unfortunately being made in ignorance of much relevant information, including alternative recommendations and the likely impact of recommendations. In other words, the advocates of PPB considered analysis a factor that should be added more systematically to the decision-making process; many felt it could improve public policy decisions.[47]

Selection of useful standards for choosing a decision-making model must also take into account that policy analysis exists in a very political, human, and practical environment.[48] Any attempt to describe properly the actual working role of policy analysis in public policymaking must consider this practical environment. Other important considerations are the advantages and disadvantages inherent in analysis,[49] since these factors will significantly influence the role of policy analysis in public policymaking. These considerations constitute the context for evaluating the relative usefulness of the various decision-making models.

Applying the above criteria to decision-making models reinforces awareness of the complexity of public policymaking. Both Lindblom's and Wildavsky's models are excellent tools for helping us understand the political environment of public policymaking, but they are not useful for explaining the more technical difficulties associated with "proper" analysis. On the other hand, the ideal rational model helps us comprehend the technical difficulties of analysis, but it is relatively useless in explaining the highly important political environment.

None of the decision-making models cited in Chapter 1, (Charles E. Lindblom's incremental change model, Aaron Wildavsky's budgetary process model, Simon's satisficing model, the ideal rational model, Dror's optimum model, or Wallen's stages of problem solving model) is adequate in terms of our criteria. However, these models taken together do help to clarify the role of policy analysis in public policymaking.

Lindblom's and Wildavsky's models are, as mentioned previously, useful in providing insight into the political context of public policymaking. Lindblom claims that "disjointed incrementalism" and "partisan mutual adjustments" best describe decision-making with respect to matters of public policy. Decisions on public policy are made at the margin rather than by comprehensive analysis, and such decisions reflect mutual partisan agreement on means rather than fundamental objectives. Wildavsky argues in the same vein by asserting that governmental budgets are decided incrementally, never by a total review of resource allocation. The decision-making process is dominated by the strategies employed and the conflicts that arise among the participants: clientele groups, agencies, departments, the Office of Management and Budget. Definable strategies exist that require such things as the agency cultivation of an active clientele, the development of confidence among other reviewing government officers such as budget examiners, and skill in following tactics that exploit temporary opportunities.[50]

The Lindblom and Wildavsky models explain the very significant fact that policy analysis must exist in a political environment. Lindblom argues against what he calls the "rational-comprehensive approach to public policy decision-making" because it is not realistic or reasonable. Wildavsky, on the other hand, argues that policy analysis is needed because it "contributes to making an agency politically and socially relevant." He does not view policy analysis as inconsistent with his thinking on the budgetary process.

The purpose of policy analysis is not to eliminate advocacy but to raise the level of argument among contending interests. If poor people want greater benefits from the government, the answer to their problems may not lie initially in policy analysis, but in political organization. Once they have organized themselves, they may want to undertake policy analysis in order to crystallize their own objectives or merely to compete with the analysis put forth by others. The end result, hopefully, would be higher quality debate and perhaps eventually public choice among better known alternatives.[51]

The use of policy analysis in urban mass-transit operating subsidy illustrates that policy analysis can be complementary to the political process, as Wildavsky asserts.

Reasoning from Lindblom's and Wildavsky's models, policy analysis must serve to aid the key actors involved in making public policy. This means that the policy analysis must be timely, must be able to be used to seize political opportunities, and must be comprehensible to those who must use the analysis in partisan bargaining situations.

The other four models—Simon's satisficing model, the ideal rational model, Dror's optimum model, and Wallen's stages of problem solving model—are helpful for understanding the nature of policy analysis itself. Simon's satisficing model serves as an alternative to the ideal rational model. Simon argues that policymakers identify alternatives until they find a satisfactory one. The search is limited by human inertia and the strength of conservative forces in the organization. The ideal rational model is in direct contrast, because the methodological goal is to search out and consider all alternatives. Secretary Volpe's decisions on the gravity vacuum train and the tracked air cushion vehicle illustrate the satisficing model. The aids to navigation decision illustrates an attempt to follow the rational model.

Both the satisficing model and the ideal rational model are useful for understanding the difficulties associated with decision-making. Simon's model dramatically emphasizes that decisions are made under pressure, and severe limitations make achieving even a satisfactory alternative a significant accomplishment. The problem with his model is that one is not being satisfied with the best alternative. On the other hand, the desire for deciding on the best alternative is reflected in the ideal rational model. The problem with that model is that it can never be achieved. We seem to be trapped between our desires for quality and the necessity to cope with our daily pressures.

Dror's optimum model is one serious attempt to deal with the dilemma illustrated by contrasting the satisficing and ideal rational model. Dror's optimum model tries to mold together the rational model, the concept of extra-rationality, and the use of analysis to decide how decisions can best be made. Dror's discussion of the optimum model points up the inadequacy of the rational model and his own desire to improve upon that model.

Wallen's stages of problem solving model is another attempt to model the salient factors of decision-making. In this model the starting point is the perception that a problem exists. By contrast to the rational model, the first factor cited is defining one's goals. Next in Wallen's model, the person proceeds to formulate the problem, define alternatives, gather information, and test proposals. In the rational model, the next steps cited are defining alternatives and gathering information. In Wallen's model, the last steps are action planning, taking action steps, and evaluating outcomes. Again in contrast, the rational model is limited to deciding a given matter based upon maximizing goals. The rational model does not extend to taking action steps and evaluating outcomes. Another distinction is that the rational model does not have reconsideration as a factor, as does Wallen's model.

Wallen's model can help us a great deal in understanding the nature of policy analysis. We know that the rational model serves as the primary theoretical explanation of how analysis should be conducted, and that the rational model cannot be attained.[52] Wallen's model can serve as an alternative theoretical explanation of how analysis should be conducted. Wallen's model permits cycles of defining one's problem, producing alternatives, and testing alternatives. It implicitly recognizes that any given analysis will depend upon the ingenuity of the analyst, the kind of data available to him, the amount of resources at his command in undertaking the analysis, and other factors discussed earlier in this chapter.

Wallen's model, coupled with the thinking of Lindblom and Wildavsky, enables us to understand that the role of policy analysis in public policymaking can be very significant, but that there are also certain very real constraints. Wallen's model helps us understand how intelligence and knowledge can be used to develop solutions to problems; and Lindblom's and Wildavsky's models help us understand the context in which this intelligence and knowledge must be used.[53]

One reason why criticisms are leveled at PPB relates to its theoretical foundation. Many individuals had false and naive expectations of PPB's capacity to improve public policymaking. The rational model, the theoretical basis of PPB, ignores the political context and demands the impossible in terms of analysis. Therefore, it is not surprising that false expectations arose, and that frustration and failures were commonly associated with PPB.[54]

Research Question

What can be expected of policy analysis as it relates to public policymaking? To consider properly this question, two correlative questions must first be addressed: What should *not* be expected of policy analysis? And in what way does policy analysis *not* relate to public policymaking?

What should *not* be expected from policy analysis? Policy analysis has its analytical limitations. A quick smooth implementation of policy analysis, particularly comprehensive and systematic attempts such as PPB, seems unlikely, especially without special resources and efforts devoted to implementation. As pointed out previously, political, human, and operational factors, such as having talented analysts, are essential. One should not expect quick success from policy analysis, but some successes may be apparent within a few months, because some beneficial analytical studies can be completed in this time. One should not expect ease in applying policy analysis to decision-making situations, because analysis is a very creative challenge, especially given the present state of the art. Also, one should not forget that policy analysis is, at best, only one factor among other considerations (such as the crisis of the moment, political implications, and the time available to make the decision) considered by decision-makers when they are making public policy decisions.

In what ways does policy analysis *not* relate to public policymaking? Many public policymaking situations do not lend themselves to assistance from policy analysis. For example, some decisions must be made in a time frame in which a useful policy analysis cannot be prepared. In other situations, adequate information for analysis might not be available or might be too costly to acquire. In some situations, the analytical ability of key decision-makers is poor; the analyst simply cannot communicate his findings, and the analysis is therefore useless. Policy analysis must serve the decision-maker by providing useful knowledge on the policy issues of the moment or by helping the decision-maker better implement his policy. Policy analysis that provides information not meeting those criteria is not relevant to public policymaking. For example, information on the number of applications processed in the year is quite irrelevant when the decision-maker wishes to give testimony on a major shift in subsidy requirements. Also, an analysis that merely explains all the disadvantages of alternative ideas without arriving at an acceptable, politically practical recommendation is not relevant to the public policymaking process. Policy analysis that does not impact the budgetary process, legislative testimony, and actions by program managers is not related to public policymaking, because these are the places where policy becomes a reality.

What can be expected of policy analysis? It can be a very helpful aid to public policymaking. It is not antithetical to the political processes as described by Lindblom and Wildavsky. It can:

1. point out to the decision-makers, in their day-to-day firehouse atmosphere, what positions are obviously foolish mistakes;
2. aid in the political bargaining process by providing greatly strengthened rationale for the policy positions, including resource allocation recommendations;
3. bring to the decision-maker pertinent information alternatives and quality thinking when he makes his decisions so that he is satisfied that he made *the best decision* under the circumstances;
4. help insure that the decision-maker's policy is implemented; and
5. help the decision-maker later reconsider his policy so that policy changes can be made based upon knowledge grained from experience.

Implications for Public Administration

The implications of this reassessment of policy analysis for day-to-day public administration is significant. Various state, local and foreign governments are considering implementing PPB.[55] In the federal government, which launched PPB in McNamara's Department of Defense, another major innovation referred to as management by objective (MBO) has just begun to be introduced. In October 1973, the Office of Management and Budget began considering how MBO could be formally incorporated into the budget process. Appropriate changes in Circular A-11, the bible of budgeting, seem quite likely.[56] It is safe to assume that there will be continued efforts to apply policy analysis and especially systematic policy analysis to governmental decision-making.

What lessons can we summarize from the federal experience with PPB?

Theoretical and Conceptual

1. Program budgeting, policy analysis, and most other related concepts are vague and contain no detailed formula for success. This does not mean that success is impossible, but only that a great deal of effort and creative talent is necessary to make these concepts operational.

2. The rational model should not be emulated as an ideal, because it encourages one to ignore critical factors such as political realities. Instead, Lindblom's, Wildavsky's, and Wallen's models should be used.

3. The use of a program structure inhibits policy analysis. Care should be taken not to apply indiscriminately the program structure, for its use seems to be limited to outlining an agency's activities.

4. Reaching organizational consensus on objectives is, at best, a very difficult undertaking. There is no one best set of objectives, for they all, by definition, involve values. In some instances, a consensus may never be reached. In framing operational objectives, broad objectives are often reinterpreted much more narrowly. This is sometimes an unavoidable situation.

5. Analysis normally is helpful only for relatively narrow but, nevertheless, important policy questions. The use of analysis is constrained by such things as the ability of the analyst and the nature of the subject being examined. Analysis is often most useful on technical questions, such as aids to navigation, rather than, for example, decisions on relative priorities.

Implementation

1. If the desire is to introduce systematic analysis into the governmental decision-making process, a significant amount of money and talent must be devoted to the effort. Highly trained people with at least the equivalent of a master's degree are essential. A training program orienting staff to the new requirements and raising skill levels of the program managers who must use analysis is necessary. A phased implementation plan should be adopted so that agencies and portions of agencies most likely to accept the changes can be introduced to the innovation first, and resisting agencies can be introduced to the changes last.

2. As a matter of realistic strategy in implementing a major administrative change like PPB, one can expect resistance from some top management

personnel which will effectively prevent successful implementation. Training and hiring policies can minimize this problem, but such effective resistance cannot be avoided entirely.

3. The key person for insuring effective policy analysis is the agency head. A desire and ability to effectively use policy analysis should be one criterion for hiring a person for this position. Then a tailor-made brief orientation course could be given new agency heads which could include the use of policy analysis in public policymaking.

4. One revealing test of effective implementation is to examine the coordination of policy among the policy analysts, the budget officer, the accountants, the lawyers, the public affairs officer, the analysts preparing the agency's progress reports, and the program managers within an agency.

Political

1. Judging by the PPB experience, policy analysis is not antithetical to the American political process, and it does not disturb the relationship between executive and legislative branches.

2. The political advantage of not using analysis with explicit objectives may be critical to reaching decisions in some specific situations, but there is no reason to believe that this is a common circumstance. In fact, a situation might occur where an analysis showing the possibility of consensus might prove to be critical to reaching a political decision.

3. The use of plans, e.g., a five-year program and financial plan, does not appear to limit the political options available.

4. Policy analysis rarely addresses the political costs and benefits of a program to specific key individuals (e.g., senators), but good analyses do address analytical questions that set out political cost and benefits in general.

Human

1. People in an agency must believe that policy analysis is significant and a legitimate undertaking. The real test for them will be how seriously key individuals (e.g., the agency head) and key agencies (e.g., the Office of Management and Budget) take policy analysis. If these groups continually demand and use analysis, then significance and legitimacy will be established.

2. Positive and politically practical recommendations must be the products of policy analysis. If these are not generated, the policy analysis unit will lose effectiveness both among its organizational peers and the key decision-makers who should use the units products.

Management

1. Systematic policy analysis does tend to centralize governmental decision-making. However, one can argue that the strong dominant personality of a high-level official may be the real reason for administrative centralization. Judging from Chapter 5, policy analysis can be used as a tool to attain some measure of centralized control. Chapters 3, 4, and 5 tend to confirm the administrative centralizing influence of PPB.

2. Judging by the material in the previous chapters, systematic policy analysis does not greatly influence reorganization through the use of a program structure or any other basis.

To further explain the implications of this reassessment of policy analysis upon public administration, a model policy analysis system and its implementation is presented. This should be considered as only one possible approach based upon the knowledge presented in these chapters. Other approaches are not only possible, but they may be more desirable under actual operating circumstances. The following merely illustrates generally how the above lessons can be applied.

Preparing for Implementation

1. The chief executive officer (president, governor, mayor) announces that (1) a policy analysis system will be implemented starting on X date, (2) the chief executive would like suggestions for its implementation, and (3) he would like volunteers for the prototype implementations. By contrast, in the federal government PPB was mandated as the system for all government agencies all at once.

2. A draft implementation strategy and an explanation of the system are circulated for comment. Changes are made in response to the comments, and temporary orders are announced for implementation in the prototype departments.

3. A vigorous training and hiring program is initiated at least one year prior to implementation. A special hiring pool of these people is created and they are assigned to the prototype departments on a temporary basis. When PPB was implemented in DOT, program analysts and economists positions were added to provide DOT with the capability to perform PPB. Training for PPB was not a common feature of PPB implementation in DOT, but the DOT experience might have been atypical. The scope of training and hiring postulated in this model was not undertaken for PPB in the Department of Transportation.

Implementation

1. Each prototype department and agency develops its own implementation strategy and system that is consistent with the guidance from higher units. This was done under PPB, as noted in Chapter 2.

2. Each group conducts its own orientation and training courses, but assistance from other units is encouraged. This was possible under PPB and did occur in the Coast Guard. In DOT, each agency was responsible for developing its own implementation strategy, but in most agencies no real systematic effort existed.

3. Implementation is done in phases:

A. A complete set of objectives is established with three levels of priorities (president, department, and agency) and specific milestones to be accomplished in the current and budget years. Ideally, the accomplishment of the objective can be verified by facts (e.g., increase transit ridership by 10% within two years).

   The presidential objectives must be approved by the president or his agent. Secretarial objectives must be approved by the secretary or his agent, and so on. The objectives and milestones should cover at least all activities for which resources must be justified in the budget process. In the Department of Transportation (except in the Coast Guard), vague long-term nonoperational objectives were established (see Chapter 2). In UMTA, the PPB objectives had little impact upon policy except for a minor role played in the project selection criteria. Use of objectives and milestones to help in the policymaking process existed only in the Coast Guard.

B. A monthly progress reporting system is then implemented with both written and oral reports given to the agency head, department head, and president (or their representatives). At the higher levels, bimonthly reports can be used. Oral sessions should concentrate on problem areas and related policy questions. Specific policy analysis papers should be used to supplement the discussions and to facilitate the decision-making process. Conscientious follow-through, such as identifying instances of poor implementation, is also important. Under PPB in the Department of Transportation, progress reports against objectives and milestones were not used. DOT agencies did have progress reporting, but it was not formally linked to PPB.

C. Integration with the budget process is next. All budget presentation must include an explanation of the resources requested in terms of specific objectives. To allocate requested resources that fulfill multiple objectives, follow the general rule of assigning as many resources as possible to the highest level objectives. General administrative expenses should be apportioned among the various objectives on some logical basis. A five-year financial plan should be included with the budget material. Policy analysis should be used to explain the rationale behind critical policy positions reflected in the budget. This was to be done under PPB.

D. The accounting system should be modified to account for expenses in terms of the objectives, as well as the traditional budgeting categories.

Under PPB, the accounting system was often linked to the program structure.

E. Program evaluation reports should focus upon the objectives and milestones. Is the objective being achieved; if not, why not? Is the strategy reflected in the milestones and financial plans the best one to achieve the objective? What improvements are needed? Is the objective itself incorrect? These questions should be addressed. Under PPB, stress was placed upon present decisions; looking at the validity of past policy decisions was not emphasized.

F. All legislation, testimony, and major speeches should be coordinated with the policy analysis unit so that policy consistency is maintained *and* supported by analysis when feasible. These policy statements often were not coordinated with the so-called "policy analysis units" that prepared the PPB documents.

Refinements and Fine-Tuning

1. Changes in objectives, schedules (called "milestones" by public administration practitioners), and procedures should be able to be made easily. At the beginning of implementation, changes should be accepted as informally as possible and in the spirit of complete cooperation. The first attempts at objectives and milestones may be poor, but stress should be placed upon getting something down that is operational. Over a period of months, improvement should be encouraged and readily accepted. After one year of operation, standards should be higher, but positive suggestions for change should continue to be accepted readily. Under PPB, most agencies tried to establish *the* system and make modifications as necessary. Often the assumption was made that refinement and fine-tuning reflected failure in the effort to establish a good system.

2. If the agency head's management style is such that he cannot operate with a policy analysis system, then either he should be fired or the system should be dropped and its resources shifted to an agency more receptive to the system. This willingness to shift resources did not exist under PPB.

3. A semiannual evaluation of the implementation should be made. Outsiders should review the agency's or department's implementation and successes. They should then make specific written recommendations for improvement. Particular attention should be focused upon the use of policy analysis by key policymakers, including such groups as the Office of Management and Budget. In the federal government attempt to institutionalize PPB, there was some evaluation of the implementation but not as comprehensive or in the form suggested here.

4. As the prototype departments and agencies become familiar with the policy analysis system, the extra personnel should be transferred out of the

departments or agencies to the next group that is starting the implementation process. This was not done under PPB.

The above model policy analysis system and its implementation builds upon the lessons learned. For example, resistance is expected, and an attempt is made to mitigate it by phasing implementation, using training, and concentrating policy analysis resources. The unique political and organizational context is accepted, and stress is placed on tailoring the system to the organization. The importance of top management using the system is recognized by starting with interested top management, evaluating success on that basis, and providing for a decision to abandon the system if the top manager cannot work with it. The political process described by Lindblom and Wildavsky is expected to continue, with the policy analysis system assisting the political bargaining process, as suggested by Wildavsky.[57]

Implications for Future Research

One of the frustrations in political science and public administration is the lack of significant sums of money to conduct research. The amount of research being conducted on the role of policy analysis in public policymaking is so small that it can be said almost not to exist. A great deal of attention to this topic has recently occurred in political science, but the research funding levels remain essentially insignificant.[58]

What can research do in this area? Policy analysis is now a largely undeveloped art form. Through research, it can be improved significantly so that policy analysis can become more relevant to the public policymaking process. The policy analyst seeks to reduce obscurantism by being explicit about problems, solutions, resources, and results. The purpose of analysis is not to eliminate advocacy but to raise the level of argument among contending interests. As mentioned before, Wildavsky points out:

If poor people want greater benefits from the government, the answer to their problems may not lie initially in policy analysis but in political organization. Once they have organized themselves, they may want to undertake policy analysis in order to crystallize their own objectives or merely to compete with the analysis put forth by others. The end result, hopefully, would be a higher quality debate and perhaps eventually public choices among better known alternatives.[59]

This role for policy analysis is unlikely without better knowledge on how to apply policy analysis to the public policymaking process.

One particularly important research focus is the relationship of policy analysis to the political process. Five topics that should be further explored are: (1) the most effective types of analysis under various typical political bargaining circumstances, (2) the usefulness of more direct analysis on political benefits and costs to key decisionmakers, (3) the effective use of analysis in the legislative process, (4) the effective use of analysis by clientele groups, and (5) the role of the analyst vis-à-vis the decision-maker.

What types of analysis are best suited to the various typical political bargaining situations? If we could categorize these types of analysis and improve their usefulness, we would go a long way toward Wildavsky's intermediate purpose of raising the quality of the debate. Possibly one type of useful analysis technique in political bargaining would be to directly assess political benefits and cost of various decisions upon key decision-makers. Would such analysis tend to improve political bargaining? Research is needed to shed light on this question. The experience with game theory in international relations should be helpful in designing the necessary research.

The use of policy analysis is mistakenly considered almost entirely as an executive branch phenomenon. Policy analysis does occur in the legislative branch, particularly in the Congressional Research Service. What are the characteristics of effective analysis in the congressional setting? This is a largely unexplored but obviously significant question related to public policymaking. Policy analysis also occurs outside traditional government in public interest groups, such as the League of Cities; foundations, such as the Ford Foundation; nonprofit organizations, such as the Brookings Institution; private interest groups, such as the National Association of Manufacturers; unions, such as the AFL-CIO; quasi-governmental groups, such as the Advisory Commission on Intergovernmental Relations, and others. How is analysis used and where is it a significant factor in policymaking? Why? These are important research questions.

Another sometimes overlooked topic is the role played by the analyst and his relationship to the decision-maker. What types of roles exist? Which are more successful and why? One complaint among analysts is that they fail to communicate properly with decision-makers. Is this true? Why? What types of communication styles are most successful? Why? Because of the highly creative nature of analysis and the importance of the decision-maker, the relationship of the analysts and the decision-maker becomes a significant factor. More knowledge about that relationship should be helpful in improving the role of policy analysis in public policymaking.

A second important research focus involves the limitations and weaknesses of policy analysis. If these can be minimized, then the role of policy analysis in public policymaking is significantly enhanced. A more sophisticated understanding of the following would be useful: (1) the significance of various styles of management by agency heads for the success of policy analysis; (2) the type of organizational data systems most supportive of policy analysis; (3) most successful ways to organizationally perceive needs, formulate the problem, create viable proposals for solution, forecast consequences and test proposals, plan actions and evaluate actions; (4) most successful strategies to integrate objective setting, progress reporting, budgeting, evaluation, and so on; and (5) most successful strategies to implement systematic policy analysis including training, overcoming organizational resistance, flexible use of talent, and evaluating the implementation.

The ingredients of analysis should be investigated to isolate better methods and determine why they are better. For example, poor data are often cited as a limitation of policy analysis. Does a good management information system, set of indicators, or other strong data base positively impact the quality of policy analysis? How can we, organizationally, through analysis, better perceive needs, formulate problems, create viable proposals for solution, forecast consequences and test proposals, plan actions, and evaluate actions? A more sophisticated understanding of these matters is needed so we can perform better analyses.

Another dimension of policy analysis, particularly systematic and comprehensive attempts such as PPB, is the integration of planning and budgeting, as well as progress reporting, program evaluation, accounting, legislative testimony, public statements, and actions of program managers. What integration strategies are most successful? Why? Public policies are goals, objectives, and missions that guide the agency. If they do guide the agency, they must be reflected and integrated into the activities listed.

The last dimension of needed research which would focus upon the limitations and weaknesses of policy analysis involves proper implementation of systematic policy analysis. One such implementation strategy was set out in the previous section of this chapter. We need to know what strategies are successful and why. What types of training are best? What are the best methods to overcome internal organizational resistance to policy analysis? Can a strategy using more talent at the beginning of the organization's learning curve be effective? What are the problems associated with this idea? What are the best methods to evaluate the implementation? These are all important research questions that will lead us to a better understanding of how we can best implement systematic policy analysis into an agency's decision-making process.

A third and final suggested research focus is the development of theories concerning the role of policy analysis in public policymaking. As pointed out earlier, the Lindblom, Wildavsky, and Wallen models taken together represent an excellent start in developing such a theory. Some obvious deficiencies not covered by the models involve the human factor, decision-making at the local levels, and decision-making at the international level. Excellent models have been developed on these topics; and in some cases, the models need only be interpreted in terms of how they add to our understanding of the ways policy analysis can better contribute to public policymaking.

Theory is meant to channel thought processes so that complex phenomena can be better understood and possibly even be manipulated to man's advantage. The literature on public policymaking and policy analysis has centered upon a clearly unsatisfactory normative model that has channeled thinking in one direction and limiteu possibilities. For example, the quixotic quest for rationality eliminates in advance our consideration of the significant political phenomenon of coalition formulation as a solution to some problems. It has discouraged us from trying a recylcing thinking process which would involve perception of the problem, problem formulation, definition of alternatives, and testing alternatives. It discourages us from considering the environment of public policymaking. Channeling thought processes is desirable if that theory or model leads to ideas that can help society better deal with its problems. However, when the theory inhibits or misdirects thinking, then that theory should be ignored and new theories developed. In the case of public policymaking and policy analysis, it is time to abandon the rational model. We should (1) build upon the Lindblom, Wildavsky and Wallen models, (2) identify other useful models from such areas of knowledge as organizational development and international relations, and (3) create new models to help us understand how we can better use policy analysis in public policymaking.

The previous few pages have touched on many of the topics needing additional research. Fortunately, with the existence of PPB in many state and local governments and the increasing likelihood that MBO will be a significant new approach to government planning and the budgeting process, there is an excellent opportunity to engage in a more sophisticated, large-scale research effort addressed to public policymaking. Unfortunately, such an effort would cost a great deal of money. As an alternative to large research efforts, individual case studies such as this one, taken collectively, might expand out understanding of the public policymaking process. A better understanding is particularly needed concerning the use of policy analysis in the various contexts in which it is now being attempted.

Appendix

Appendix
Excerpts from U.S. Coast
Guard PPB Manual

The following excerpts, from the U.S. Coast Guard *Planning and Programming Manual–1971*, are cited to further clarify and explain PPB in the Coast Guard.

A. Purpose and Scopes of Manual

This manual briefly sets forth staff responsibilities, procedures and time tables for actions involved in the Planning and Programming cycle of the Coast Guard.

Parts I, II, and III are designed to give a degree of familiarity with the concepts involved in the cycle. Part IV and the appendices develop procedures for those more intimately involved in the production of necessary documentation, and Part V describes the programs.

B. Definitions

In August 1965, the President of the United States prescribed that the major Federal departments and agencies adopt a Planning-Programming-Budgeting (PPB) system which had been instituted, with good results, in the Department of Defense in 1961.

In essence, PPB calls for:

1. Designing for each government agency an output-oriented program structure under which data on all operations and activities can be presented in categories that reflect the agency's purpose or objectives.
2. Making analyses, in terms of costs, effectiveness and benefits of possible alternatives for meeting agency program objectives.
3. Translating decisions on programs into financial budgets for consideration and action by the President and the Congress with subsequent devising of operating budgets for management control purposes.

In general, documented objectives, criteria, and benefits become a significant part of the analytical process to aid higher authority in arriving at informed judgement on alternative courses of action and assist in establishing program priorities within limited resources. Also, much improved coordination is achieved in developing viable long-range plans which are essentially valid over a period of years, yet amenable to annual adjustment.

The following list of definitions will orient the reader to the vocabulary of the Planning, Programming and Budgeting System.

AC&I Project Proposal Reports. A submission on specified forms by a District or Headquarters Unit describing a capital investment in facilities. The AC&I Project Proposal Report is used for approval of details of a project and for engineering sufficiency.

Benefits. Measures of attainment expressed in terms of the broad objectives.

Determinations. A statement of assumptions, points of emphasis and unresolved areas from the Program Manager through his Program Director to the Chief of Staff for approval/resolution by the Commandant as a planning guide for the program.

Development Plan (DP). A submission to Headquarters by a district or Headquarters Unit involving a major facility investment that will require costly multi-year funding with completion through a series of phases over a period of years. For units designated by Headquarters, a Master Plan meets the Planning Proposal and Development Plan requirements.

Goal. The program level to be attained within described budgetary limitations in any fiscal period that effectively supports the program objectives. (May be expressed in general terms or a percentage; e.g., maintain LORAN C coverage integrity 99% of the time; or inspect each waterfront facility at least once each six months.)

Input. The total resources including personnel, funds and facilities required or utilized to obtain a specific output.

Long Range View. The Long Range View is a broad statement embodying a set of assumptions which identifies where the Coast Guard intends to be ten years hence. As such it provides the orientation and basis for current and intermediate decisions and actions.

Major Program Issues (MPI). Particular issues on which the Office of Management and Budget requests specific attention in the Program Memorandum. In some instances, the Coast Guard may be the sole bureau in the Department that is concerned while in other instances, the Coast Guard will contribute toward an issue cutting across the lines of several bureaus.

Objective. The broad purpose toward which each program of the Coast Guard is directed. Among the other things, safety, economic efficiency, and increase in the benefits derived in aesthetic, social, and environmental values are generally included. The Coast Guard program objective supports the Departmental objectives for the category in which the Coast Guard program is included.

Operating Program Manager. The Division Chief in the district office who is immediately responsible under the District Commander for the overall management of a program within the district. For example, the Chief, Merchant Marine Safety Division in a district is the Operating Program Manager for Commercial Vessel Safety Program.

Output. Measures which are usually expressed in physical terms of what a program produces directly. Examples are: numbers of merchant vessel inspections, numbers of oceanographic stations occupied, and numbers of courtesy motorboat examinations performed by the Coast Guard Auxiliary. Outputs should not be confused with benefits. The outputs are intended to result in benefits.

Planning Factors. Information distributed by Headquarters to districts and Headquarters Units, which are allotment units, on which their field budget requests are based.

Planning Proposal. A submission from a district or a Headquarters Unit recommending change to existing plans or facilities. Precedes the submission of a DP or AC&I Project Proposal Report. For units designated by Headquarters, a Master Plan meets the planning and development plan requirements.

Plan Summary. A summary of a plan of an individual program for the near-term (1-5 years), mid-term (6-10 years) and long-term (10 years and beyond).

Program (noun). A major Coast Guard endeavor, mission-oriented, which fulfills statutory or executive requirements, and which is defined in terms of the principle actions required to achieve a significant end objective.

Program (verb). The process of deciding on specific courses of action to be followed in carrying out planning decisions on objectives. Also involved are decisions in terms of total costs to be incurred over a period of years as to personnel, material, and financial resources to be applied in carrying out programs.

Program Category. The first level of breakdown in the Departmental program structure. The categories provide the framework on which major questions of mission and scale of operations are presented to higher levels of Departmental management and the Executive Office of the President. An example in the Department of Transportation is Inter-Urban Transportation.

Program Cost Categories:

Research & Development Costs. Those program costs incurred under the RDT&E appropriation where the intended end item will lead to acquisition of new equipment for operational use, or will result in innovative changes in the conduct of a mission.

Investment Costs. Those program costs to procure or construct initial, additional or replacement equipment or facilities, or to provide for major modifications to existing facilities. These are represented by the Coast Guard's Acquisition, Construction and Improvement projects.

Operating Costs. Those program costs required to operate and maintain a capability.

Program Data Summary (PDS). The document, submitted along with the PP for each program, which provides the input for the Departmental PFP.

Program Definition. The Definition describes a program in terms of objectives, measures of output and benefits, OPFAC resources employed and methods of determining cost benefits and cost-effectiveness as well as the management information data required.

Program Director. The flag officer at Headquarters immediately responsible to the Commandant for the overall management of a program. He has responsibility for the accomplishment of program objectives effectively and efficiently through short- and long-range planning/programming of personnel and material resources for the program.

Program Element. The third level in the Departmental program structure. It is at this level that the Coast Guard manages its programs and supports them to the Department. For example, Short-Range Aids to Navigation is an element under Inter-Urban Transportation: Water.

Program Financial Plan (PFP). A tabular form submission made by the Department to the Office of Management and Budget that provides data for each program relating outputs, benefits, costs and personnel for the current year, the preceding year, the budget year, and four following years.

Program Manager. The staff officer at Headquarters designated by and responsible to the Program Director for the detailed management of a Coast Guard program.

Program Memorandum (PM). A narrative submission by the Department to the Office of Management and Budget which is oriented to the major issues of the Departments. It discusses objectives, alternatives considered and the rationale supporting a preferred course of action.

Program Proposal (PP). A narrative submission by the Coast Guard to the Department for each program element. The Program Proposal discusses objectives, alternatives; reasons for preferred alternatives, necessary legislation and impact if the change is not accepted. The PP is self-contained and includes all necessary backup information or references to studies. As such, the PP provides much of the input for the Department PM.

Program Subcategory. The secondary level in the Departmental program structure. The subcategories provide a meaningful substantive breakdown of program categories. Under Inter-Urban Transportation the subcategory Water is of immediate interest to the Coast Guard.

Resource Change Proposal (RCP). The document prepared by the Program Manager and submitted via the Program Director to the Chief of Staff (CPA), is used for requesting a change in program resources. The change may reflect an increase or decrease in a program or a shift of resources from one program to another. The RCP does not replace the change in Financial Plan used for funding adjustments within appropriations during the operating year.

Special Analytic Studies (SAS). These studies provide the basis for decision reflected in the PM. Some will be completed in one budget year while some will extend beyond a single cycle. The continuing study will develop on a longer run basis the conceptual understanding necessary to improve the data available and to provide an analytic basis for deciding future Major Program Issues. The Department will structure and monitor these and in some instances perform the study, while in other cases the Coast Guard may provide input or conduct the entire study.

Study Manager. That person designated by proper authority, in a precept, to perform a study, or direct a study group.

Support Director. Support Directors are responsible to the Program Directors for actual administration of funds, providing dollar estimates, for design characteristics, maintenance of facilities, training, assignment and payment of personnel, and other logistical functions.

Support Manager. The staff officer at Headquarters designated by and responsible to the Support Director for the detailed management of the Support Program.

Support Program Manager. The Chief, Engineering, Comptroller, and Personnel Divisions in the district office. Their relationship to the Operating Program Manager is similar to that between the Program Director/Manager and Support Director/Manager at Headquarters.

Notes

Notes

Notes to Preface

1. Yehezkel Dror, *Public Policymaking Re-Examined* (San Francisco: Chandler Publishing Company, 1968), p. 271.

Chapter 1
PPB and the Research Question

1. Fremont J. Lyden and Ernest G. Miller, eds., *Planning-Programming-Budgeting: A Systems Approach to Management* (Chicago: Markham Publishing Company, 1967), p. 5.

2. Frederick C. Mosher, "New Integrated Systems for Planning, Programming and Budgeting" (paper prepared for the XVth International Congress of Administrative Science, 1971), p. 1.

3. Harold D. Lasswell, *Politics: Who Gets What, When, How* (New York: McGraw-Hill Book Co., 1936).

4. David Easton, *The Political System* (New York: Alfred A. Knopf, 1953), p. 129.

5. Lyden and Miller, *Planning-Programming-Budgeting*, p. 5.

6. Ibid.

7. Arthur Smithies, *The Budgetary Process in the United States* (New York: McGraw-Hill Book Co., Inc., 1955).

8. Jesse Burkhead, *Government Budgeting* (New York: John Wiley and Sons, Inc., 1965).

9. David Novick, *Efficiency and Economy in Government Through New Budgeting and Accounting Procedures* (Santa Monica, Calif.: The Rand Corporation, 1954), R-254; Novick, *A New Approach to the Military Budget* (Santa Monica, Calif.: The Rand Corporation, 1956), RM-1759; and Novick, ed., *Program Budgeting* (Cambridge, Mass.: Harvard University Press, 1965).

10. Werner Z. Hirsch, "Toward Federal Program Budgeting," *Public Administration Review* 26 (December 1966): 259.

11. Bertram M. Gross, "The New Systems Budgeting," *Public Administration Review* 29 (March/April 1969): 113.

12. Allen Schick, "The Road to PPB: The Stages of Budget Reform," *Public Administration Review* 26 (December 1966): 244.

13. New York Bureau of Municipal Research, *Making a Municipal Budget* (New York: Bureau of Municipal Research, 1907).

14. Aaron Wildavsky, "The Political Economy of Efficiency: Cost-Benefit Analysis, Systems Analysis and Program Budgeting," *Public Administration Review* 26 (December 1966): 307.

15. U.S. Congress, Senate, Subcommittee on National Security and International Affairs, *Planning-Programming-Budgeting, Hearings*, before a subcommittee of the Committee on Government Operations, Senate, 90th Cong., 1st sess., 1967, p. 43.

16. Harry P. Hatry and John F. Cotton, *Program Planning for State, County and City* (Washington, D.C.: State-Local Finance Project of George Washington University, 1967), p. 15.

17. Schick, "Road to PPB," p. 253.

18. Gross, "New Systems Budgeting," p. 120.

19. Schick, "Road to PPB," p. 254.

20. See "Comparison of Old and New Budget Concepts, Special Analysis A," *U.S. Budget, FY 1969.*

21. See "Investment, Operating and Other Budget Outlays, Special Analysis D," *U.S. Budget, FY 1969.*

22. Gross, "New Systems Budgeting," p. 121.

23. Schick, "Road to PPB," p. 255.

24. Gross, "New Systems Budgeting," p. 122.

25. E.S. Quade, "Systems Analysis Techniques for Planning-Programming-Budgeting," in *Planning-Programming-Budgeting*, ed. by Fremont J. Lyden and Ernest G. Miller (2nd ed.; Chicago: Markham Publishing Company, 1972), pp. 245-46.

26. Gross, "New Systems Budgeting," p. 125.

27. Schick, "Road to PPB," p. 255, and the White House Press Release, 12 March 1970.

28. Schick, "Road to PPB," p. 244.

29. William A. Capron, "The Impact of Analysis on Bargaining in Government," in *Politics, Programs, and Budgets*, ed. by James W. Davis, Jr. (Englewood Cliffs, N.J.: Prentice-Hall, 1969), p. 257.

30. Capron, "The Impact of Analysis," p. 255.

31. Chester Wright and Michael D. Tate, *Economics and Systems Analysis: Introduction for Public Managers* (Reading, Mass.: Addison-Wesley Publishing Company, 1973), p. 140.

32. Ibid., p. vi.

33. Capron, "The Impact of Analysis," p. 258.

34. Charles E. Lindblom, "The Science of 'Muddling Through,' " *Public Administration Review* 19, no. 2 (Spring 1959): 79-88.

35. Dror, *Public Policymaking Re-Examined* (San Francisco: Chandler Publishing Company, 1968).

36. Aaron Wildavsky, *The Politics of the Budgetary Process* (Boston: Little, Brown, 1964).

37. Herbert A. Simon, *Models of Man* (New York: John Wiley and Sons, 1957), p. 291; James G. March and Herbert A. Simon, *Organization* (New York: John Wiley and Sons, 1958), p. 136. See Dror, *Public Policymaking Re-*

Examined, Appendix D, for a more complete discussion of the literature on this and the other models.

38. Dror, *Public Policymaking Re-Examined*, p. 132.

39. Ibid., p. 152.

40. Ibid., pp. 154-62.

41. Edgar H. Schein, *Process Consultation: Its Role in Organization Development* (Reading, Mass.: Addison-Wesley Publishing Company, 1969), p. 46.

42. Ibid. The basic model was developed by Richard Wallen and is discussed fully by Schein.

43. Schein, *Process Consultation*, p. 46.

44. Ibid.

45. Capron, "The Impact of Analysis," p. 254.

Chapter 2
PPB in the Department of Transportation

1. U.S., Office of Management and Budget, Bulletin No. 68-9, 12 April 1968.

2. Allen Schick, "A Death in the Bureaucracy: The Demise of Federal PPB," *Public Administration Review* 33 (March/April, 1973): 146.

3. U.S., Department of Transportation, "DOT Planning-Programming-Budgeting System," *Order* DOT 2400.2A, 15 January 1968.

4. U.S., Department of Transportation, "FY 1973 Planning and Budgeting Process," *Notice* DOT 5100.1, 29 June 1971.

5. DOT *Order* 2400.2A.

6. DOT *Order* 2400.2A.

7. Ibid., p. 3.

8. U.S., Department of Transportation, Urban Mass Transportation Administration, "UMTA Planning-Programming-Budgeting System," UMTA *Order* 2400.1, 12 December 1969.

9. Ibid., p. 1.

10. Ibid.

11. Ibid.

12. U.S., Department of Transportation, Coast Guard, *Planning and Programming Manual—1971*, January 1971, p. I-1.

13. Ibid., p. III-3. See Appendix.

14. Ibid.

15. Interview with Coast Guard officer formerly working in PPB, 12 November 1971. The names of nearly all interviewees in this book have been kept confidential.

16. Coast Guard *Manual*.

17. Interviews with the Office of Planning and Program Review employee on 7 November 1971, former employee of the Office of Planning and Program Review on 1 November, and personal conclusions.

18. Interview with former Office of Planning and Program Review employee, 3 November 1971.

19. Ibid.

20. Author's observations based on working in UMTA three years.

Chapter 3
Research on Urban Transportation

1. *Urban Mass Transportation Act of 1964*, as revised 78 *Stat.* 302, 49 U.S.C. 1601 *et seq.* (1972).

2. John F. Burby, "Urban Report/Mass Transit Agency Faces Planning Problems in Shift from Rags to Riches," *National Journal* 2, no. 40 (3 October 1970): 2153.

3. Author's observations based upon several years' work in UMTA, 1969-71.

4. Interview with UMTA employee, 18 October 1971.

5. Ibid.; see also Burby, "Urban Report."

6. Author's observations; see also Burby, "Urban Report."

7. Burby, "Urban Report."

8. Ibid.

9. Ibid.

10. Author's conclusions.

11. Interviews with UMTA employees who worked on the service development projects over several years, 18 October and 8 November 1971.

12. Author's observations.

13. Interview with senior UMTA employee involved in RD&D projects, 15 December 1971.

14. Victor Cohn, "U.S. Seeks New Ways to Improve Transport," *Washington Post*, 3 February 1972.

15. Author's observations and conclusions.

16. Author's conclusions.

17. U.S., Congress, Senate, Committee on Banking and Currency, *Report* to accompany S.3700 together with individual views (Urban Mass Transportation Amendments of 1966), 8 August 1966 (Washington, D.C.: U.S. Government Printing Office, 1966); Public Law 89-562, 89th Cong., 2d sess., 8 September 1966.

18. Henry S. Reuss, "Research is Needed to Develop New Modes of Urban Transport," *Transportation Journal* 5 (Winter 1965): 24.

19. Henry S. Reuss, "A Breakthrough in New Urban Transport Systems," *Traffic Quarterly* 20 (January 1966): 25.

20. Reuss, "Research is Needed," p. 24.

21. David G. Lawrence, *The Politics of Innovation in Urban Mass Transportation Policy Making: The New System Example* (Washington, D.C.: National Technical Information Service PB 194 098, August 1970), p. 7; also interview with UMTA employee, 6 October 1971 and interview with former HUD employee, 13 December 1974.

22. Lawrence, *Politics of Innovation*, p. 12.

23. Ibid., p. 14.

24. Ibid., p. 15.

25. Ibid., p. 17.

26. Ibid., p. 18.

27. Public Law 89-562, 89th Congress, 2nd Session.

28. Interview, 6 October 1971.

29. Lawrence, *Politics of Innovation*, p. 42.

30. Interview, 6 October 1971.

31. Ibid.

32. Lawrence, *Politics of Innovation*, p. 42.

33. Interview, 21 December 1971.

34. Interview, 15 December 1971.

35. Ibid.; also interview with high-level UMTA employee, 4 November 1971.

36. Interviews cited in preceding note.

37. Interview, 4 November 1971.

38. Ibid.; Ray Herbert, "Air Cushion Train Plan Hits Board Roadblock," *Los Angeles Times*, 5 November 1971; and U.S., Congress, House, Subcommittee on Transportation, *Reprogramming for the Dulles TACV Demonstration Project, Hearings*, before a subcommittee of the Committee on Appropriations, House, 92d Cong., 1st Sess. (23 March 1971), vol. I, p. 396.

39. Interview, 4 November 1971.

40. U.S. Congress, House, Appropriations Subcommittee on Transportation, *Hearings*, 23 March 1971.

41. Ibid.

42. Interview, 15 December 1971.

43. Interview with senior UMTA employee, 10 December 1971; also interview, 21 December 1971.

44. Interview, 21 December 1971.

45. Representative Joel T. Broyhill, letter to Secretary John Volpe, 8 March 1971.

46. Senator William B. Spong, Jr., letter to Secretary John Volpe, 2 April 1972.

47. U.S. Congress, House, Appropriations Subcommittee on Transportation, *Hearings* 23 March 1971.

48. Author's observations; Cohn, "U.S. Seeks New Ways."

Chapter 4
Urban Mass Transportation Subsidies

1. Urban Mass Transportation Assistance Act of 1964 as amended through 15 October 1970, 78 *Stat.* 302 (October 15, 1970), 49 U.S.C. 1601 *et seq.* (October 15, 1970).

2. Based on author's conversations with an UMTA official shortly after the legislation was passed.

3. William Lilley III, "Urban Report/Urban Interests Win Transit Bill with 'Letter Perfect' Lobbying," *National Journal* 9 September 1970, p. 2021.

4. Ibid.

5. Interview with UMTA employee, 13 December 1971.

6. Lilley, "Urban Interests Win," p. 2028; interviews with Fred Burke, 30 November 1971, and with UMTA employee, 13 December 1971, confirmed the *National Journal* article.

7. Lilley, "Urban Interests Win," p. 2029.

8. Ibid., p. 2026.

9. Ibid., p. 2029.

10. Based on author's conversations with an UMTA official while this legislation was being considered.

11. Lilley, "Urban Interests Win," p. 2028.

12. Interview with UMTA employee, 13 December 1971.

13. Ibid.

14. Albert R. Karr, "Transit Boosters Complain that Administration Is Holding Back Funds Already Okayed by Congress," *Wall Street Journal*, 24 December 1971; Institute of Rapid Transit, *Digest*, no. 8 (January-February 1972), p. 4.

15. Author's conclusions. The author worked more than three years in the office that prepared the material cited.

16. Thomas D. Lynch, "Federal Capital Assistance for Transit Systems," memorandum to Milton L. Brooks, August 1971, based on information provided by applicants requesting assistance.

17. Ibid.

18. UMTA responses *re* budget request, 6 October 1971.

19. Requested for spring previews of FY 1973 and 1974.

20. Lynch, "Federal Capital Assistance."

21. Responses by UMTA to OMB questions on UMTA's budget request, 6 October 1971.

22. In the spring previews of FY 1973 and 1974, policy papers were requested on such topics as the extent "to which the Federal Government can and should subsidize the construction of major new transit systems."

23. Robert P. Mayo, letter to John Volpe, 2 February 1970, included in UMTA, "Preliminary Report on Criteria and Objectives for UMTA Programs: A Special Analytical Study for the Bureau of the Budget," June 1970.

24. UMTA, "Preliminary Report."

25. Observations of the author.

26. UMTA, "Preliminary Report."

27. Observation of author.

28. American Transit Association, *Bulletin*, 28 July 1971.

29. Observations by author.

30. C.C. Villarreal, memorandum to key UMTA, DOT and OMB staff transmitting the draft study, 12 November 1970.

31. Author's conclusion.

32. Villarreal, memorandum to key UMTA, DOT and OMB staff, 12 November 1970.

33. C.C. Villarreal, memorandum to John Ollson transmitting the final draft of "Criteria and Objectives for the UMTA Program," 17 December 1970.

34. Donald B. Rice, Assistant Director of OMB, "OMB Recommendations Concerning Criteria and Objectives for UMTA Programs," memorandum to Undersecretary James Beggs, 9 February 1971.

35. C.C. Villarreal, "OMB Recommendations Concerning Criteria and Objectives for UMTA Programs," memorandum to James Beggs, 16 February 1971.

36. James Beggs, "Criteria and Objectives for UMTA Programs," memorandum to Donald B. Rice, 17 February 1971.

37. Robert McManus, "Implementing Revised Criteria and Objectives for UMTA Capital Grant Program," Draft memorandum from C.C. Villarreal to John Ollson, 17 April 1971.

38. "Dozen Cities Planning or Building Transit Lines," *New York Times*, 29 January 1972; C.C. Villarreal, "UMTA Capital Grant Objective and Criteria," memorandum to James Beggs, n.d.

39. *Congressional Record*, 1 February 1972, S-892. Speech inserted into the record by Senator Allott. The speech by Carlos Villarreal was delivered before the 51st annual meeting of the Highway Research Board in Washington, D.C., 19 January 1972.

40. Informal conversations with Robert McManus in October 1971 and Edward Harper (White House, Domestic Council) in 1971.

41. James Beggs, "Criteria and Objectives for the UMTA Program," memorandum to Donald B. Rice, 30 April 1971.

42. Gordon Murray, letter to William R. MacDougall, 29 June 1971.

43. Gordon Murray, "Meeting on Capital Grant Criteria," note to C.C. Villarreal, 12 July 1971.

44. American Transit Association, *Bulletin* 28 July 1971.

45. Interview with Fred Burke, 30 November 1971.

46. Senator Henry M. Jackson, letter to Secretary John Volpe, 2 July 1971; and Secretary John Volpe, letter to Senator Henry M. Jackson, 5 August 1971.

47. Robert McManus, "Status of the New Criteria and/or Evaluation of Capital Grant Criteria," memorandum to William Allison, 5 October 1971.

48. Robert McManus, "Revision of the UMTA Capital Grant Criteria," memorandum to William Hurd, 14 March 1972; McManus, memorandum on same subject to Fred Meister of OMB, 14 March 1972.

49. Robert McManus, "UMTA Capital Grant Objectives and Criteria," memorandum drafted from C.C. Villarreal to James Beggs, 24 April 1972; American Transit Association, *Passenger Transport*, 2 June 1972, p. 1.

50. Robert Prestemon, "Program Issues for the FY 1974 Program Planning and Budgeting Process (Spring Preview)," memorandum to UMTA, 21 March 1972.

51. Author's notes of the meeting.

52. Urban Mass Transportation Assistance Act of 1964 as amended through October 15, 1970, 78 *Stat*. 302 (October 15, 1970), 49 U.S.C. 1601 *et seq*. (October 15, 1970).

53. *Washington Post*, 1 February 1972; American Transit Association, *Passenger Transport*, 4 February 1972, p. 1.

54. William Lilley III, "Urban Report/Transit Lobby Sights Victory in Fight for Massive Subsidy Program," *National Journal* XL, 4 March 1972, pp. 393-403.

55. U.S., Department of Transportation, "Feasibility of Federal Assistance to Urban Mass Transportation Operating Costs," 22 November 1971.

56. Ibid.

57. Author's observations.

58. Lilley, "Transit Lobby Sights Victory," p. 394.

59. Interview with Fred Burke, 30 November 1971.

60. McManus, "UMTA Capital Criteria."

61. Interview with Fred Burke, 30 November 1971.

62. Jack Anderson, "The Washington Merry-Go-Round," *Washington Post*, 9 November 1972, p. B9.

63. Interview with Fred Burke, 30 November 1971.

64. Lilley, "Transit Lobby Sights Victory," p. 397.

65. C.C. Villarreal, "Task Force Re: Transit Assistance Grants," memorandum to deputy undersecretary and others, 17 December 1971.

66. Robert McManus, "Discussion Paper, Alternative Operating Grant Program," memorandum to C.C. Villarreal, 24 January 1972.

67. C.C. Villarreal, "Report on Alternative Assistance Programs," memorandum to deputy undersecretary and others, 11 February 1972.

68. Interview with Fred Burke, 30 November 1971.

69. Lilley, "Transit Lobby Sights Victory," p. 397.

70. Ibid.

71. Jack Eisen, "Transit Leaders Plead for Subsidy at Senate Hearing," *Washington Post*, 1 February 1972.

72. American Transit Association, *Passenger Transport*, 4 February 1972.

73. "Transit Subsidy Approved," *Washington Post*, 17 February 1972.

74. Robert Lindsey, "U.S. Is Considering Mass Transit Aid," *New York Times*, 2 February 1972; Institute of Rapid Transit, *Digest* (March-April 1972), p. 6.

75. American Transit Association, *Passenger Transport*, 25 February 1972.

76. Lilley, "Transit Lobby Sights Victory," p. 400.

77. American Transit Association, *Passenger Transport*, 3 March 1972; *Congressional Record*, S-3103, 2 March 1972. Floor debate on the Housing and Urban Development Act of 1972.

78. American Transit Association, *Passenger Transport*, 3 March 1972; George Haley (UMTA Chief Counsel), "Senate Urban Mass Transportation Amendments," memorandum to C.C. Villarreal, 3 March 1972.

79. Draft House committee bill circulated to UMTA in early March 1972.

80. William Lilley III, "Urban Report/Transit Lobby Sights Victory in Fight for Massive Subsidy Program," *National Journal* XL, 4 March 1972, p. 404. Reprinted by permission.

81. Secretary John Volpe, "Mass Transit Operating Assistance," memorandum to Ehrlichman and Shultz, 7 April 1972.

82. Eisen, "Transit Leaders Plead for Subsidy."

83. Robert McManus, "Testimony on Federal Mass Transit Operating Subsidies," memorandum to Barclay Webber (DOT general counsel in charge of legislative testimony), 5 June 1972.

84. American Transit Association, *Passenger Transport*, 16 June 1972.

Chapter 5
Aids to Navigation

1. Interview with Coast Guard employee, 24 May 1972.

2. Interview with Coast Guard employee, 25 June 1972.

3. Interview, 24 May 1972.

4. Interview, 25 June 1972.

5. Interview, 24 May 1972.

6. Interview with Coast Guard employee, 18 August, 1972.

7. Ibid.

8. Interview, 25 June 1972.

9. U.S., Department of Transportation, Coast Guard, "Status of Systems Study of Short-Range Aids to Navigation," unpublished paper, 1 June 1972.

10. Interview, 24 May 1972.

11. Interview with Coast Guard employee, 14 June 1972; Coast Guard, "Status of Systems Study."

12. Interviews, 24 May, 14 June, and 18 August 1972; Coast Guard, "Status of Systems Study."

13. Interview, 18 August 1972.

14. Interview, 24 May 1972.

15. Ibid.

16. Interview with employee of Office of the Secretary, Department of Transportation, 24 August 1972.

17. Interview, 24 May 1972.

18. Interview, 24 August 1972.

19. U.S., Department of Transportation, *National Plan for Navigation*, May 1970.

20. Ibid., p. 14.

21. Ibid.,

22. Ibid., p. 16; interviews, 24 May and 25 June 1972.

23. DOT, *National Plan for Navigation*, May 1970, p. 17.

24. Interview with Coast Guard employee, 28 July 1972; also interviews, 18 and 24 August 1972.

25. Interviews, 25 June and 28 July.

26. Interview, 24 August, 1972.

27. Interview, 28 July 1972.

28. Interview, 24 August 1972.

29. Ibid.

30. Interview, 28 July 1972.

31. Interview with employee of Office of the Secretary, Department of Transportation, 7 August 1972; also interviews, 25 June and 28 July 1972.

32. Interview, 24 August 1972.

33. Interviews, 24 May, 14 and 25 June, 28 July, 7, 18, and 29 August 1972.

34. Interview, 25 June 1972.

35. Interviews, 18 and 24 August 1972.

36. Ibid.

37. U.S., Department of Transportation, *National Plan for Navigation*, April 1972. Document is available from the National Technical Information Service, Springfield, Virginia, 22151.

38. Interviews, 25 June and 18 August 1972.

39. Interviews, 24 May, 14 and 25 June, 28 July, and 7, 18, and 29 August 1972.

40. H.D. Muth, acting chief, Office of Marine Environment and Systems, "FY 1974 Budget Planning Cycle," memorandum to Aids to Navigation Division, 17 August 1971.

41. Chief of Staff, "Plans for Major Projects for Short-Range Aids to Navigation," memorandum to the chief, Office of Operations, 19 July 1971.

42. Chief, Office of Marine Environment and Systems, "Format and Content of Plan Summary for Short-Range A/N," memorandum to the Division of Plans Evaluation, August 1971.

43. U.S., Department of Transportation, Coast Guard, "FY 1974 Plan Summary for Short-Range Aids to Navigation," n.d.

44. U.S., Department of Transportation, Coast Guard, *Planning and Programming Manual*, p. IV-8.

45. Commandant, "FY 1974 Program Determinations," memorandum to program managers, 10 January 1972.

46. Ibid.

47. Coast Guard *Manual*; interviews, 7 and 18 August 1972.

48. Coast Guard *Manual*.

49. U.S., Department of Transportation, Coast Guard, *FY 1973 Spring Preview*, 22 June 1971.

50. Interview, 14 June 1972.

51. U.S., Department of Transportation, Coast Guard, *FY 1973 Spring Preview*.

52. Commandant, "FY 1974 Program Guidance," memorandum, 13 July 1972.

Chapter 6
Policy Analysis and Public Policymaking

1. Question and answer session held at a meeting of the National Capital Area Chapter, American Society for Public Administration, George Washington University, Washington, D.C. 24 April 1973.

2. Capron, "The Impact of Analysis on Bargaining in Government," p. 254.

3. Alain C. Enthoven, "The System Analysis Approach" in *Program Budgeting and Benefit-Cost Analysis*, ed. by Harley H. Hinrichs and Graeme M. Taylor (Pacific Palisades, Calif.: Goodyear Publishing Co., 1969), pp. 159-67; Charles J. Hitch and Roland N. McKean, *The Economics of Defense in the Nuclear Age* (New York: Atheneum, 1970), p. 1; and Charles L. Schultz, "Statement of Charles L. Schultz, Director, Bureau of the Budget" in *Politics, Programs and Budgets*, ed. by James W. Davis, Jr. (Englewood Cliffs, N.J.: Prentice Hall, 1969), pp. 187-99.

4. Capron, "The Impact of Analysis on Bargaining in Government," p. 254.

5. Aaron Wildavsky, *The Politics of the Budgetary Process*; Richard F. Fenno, "The Impact of PPBS on the Congressional Appropriation Process," in *Information Support, Program Budgeting and the Congress*, ed. by Robert T. Chartrand, Kenneth Janda, and Michael Hugo (New York: Spartan Books, 1968), pp. 184-85; Peter Woll, *American Bureaucracy* (New York: W.W. Norton and Company, Inc., 1963).

6. Joon Chien Doh, *The Planning-Programming-Budgeting System in Three Federal Agencies* (Washington, D.C.: Praeger Publishers, 1971), p. 115.

7. This is discussed in relationship to PPB in Edwin L. Harper, et al., "The Implementation and Use of PPB in Sixteen Federal Agencies," *Public Administration Review* 29 (November/December 1969): 632.

8. Doh, *PPB System*, p. 111; Capron, "The Impact of Analysis on Bargaining in Government," p. 266.

9. U.S., Congress, Joint Economic Committee, *The Analysis and Evaluation of Public Expenditure: The PPB System*, a compendium of papers submitted to the Subcommittee on Economy in Government (Washington, D.C.: U.S. Government Printing Office, 1969), vol. I, p. 7.

10. U.S., Congress, Senate, Committee on Government Operations, "Program Budgeting in Foreign Affairs: Some Reflections," by Frederick C. Mosher, prepared for the Subcommittee on National Security and International Organizations (Washington, D.C.: U.S. Government Printing Office, 1970), p. 22.

11. Interviews with Coast Guard Officers.

12. U.S., Congress, Senate, Committee on Government Operations, *Program Budgeting in Foreign Affairs: Some Reflections*, memorandum prepared at the request of the Subcommittee on National Security and International Operations, pursuant to S. Res. 212, 90th Cong., 2nd Session (Washington: U.S. Government Printing Office, 1968).

13. Doh, *PPB System*, p. 38.

14. Ibid., p. 29.

15. Ibid., pp. 22, 25, 32, 35, 95, 98.

16. Aaron Wildavsky, "Rescuing Policy Analysis from PPB" in *Public Expenditures and Policy Analysis*, ed. by Robert H. Haveman and Julius Margolis (Chicago: Markham Publishing Company, 1972), pp. 468-71.

17. Ibid., p. 468.

18. Ibid., pp. 469-70.

19. Ibid., p. 471.

20. Allen Schick, "A Death in the Bureaucracy: The Demise of Federal PPB," *Public Administration Review* 33 (March/April 1973): 148.

21. Capron, "The Impact of Analysis on Bargaining in Government," p. 266.

22. Memorandum from the President to the Heads of Departments and Agencies on the Government-Wide Planning, Programming, and Budgeting System, 17 November 1966, in Davis, *Politics, Programs, and Budgets*, p. 161.

23. Schick, "Demise of PPB," p. 149.

24. Ibid.

25. Wildavsky, "The Political Economy of Efficiency," pp. 230-52.

26. Capron, "The Impact of Analysis on Bargaining in Government," p. 263.

27. Ibid., p. 262.

28. Ibid., p. 254.

29. This was raised as a proposal for discussion at the Washington, D.C. Chapter Conference of The Institute for Management Science in Gaithersburg, Maryland, October 1969.

30. Capron, "The Impact of Analysis on Bargaining in Government," p. 254.

31. Wildavsky, "The Political Economy of Efficiency," pp. 244, 245.

32. Capron, "The Impact of Analysis on Bargaining in the Government," p. 259.

33. Ibid., p. 260.

34. Committee for Economic Development, *Improving Economic Management in the Federal Government* (New York: Committee for Economic Development, July 1964), p. 23.

35. David T. Stanley, et al., *Men Who Govern: A Biographical Profile of Political Executives* (Washington, D.C.: Brookings Institution, 1967).

36. For example, Leonard Merewitz and Stephen H. Sosnick, *The Budget's New Clothes* (Chicago: Markham Publishing Company, 1971), and Harley H. Hinrichs and Graeme M. Taylor, *Program Budgeting and Benefit-Cost Analysis* (Pacific Palisades, Calif.: Goodyear Publishing Co., Inc., 1969).

37. Merewitz and Sosnick, *Budget's New Clothes*, pp. 9-12, 73-108.

38. Hoos, *Systems Analysis*, pp. 136-39.

39. Merewitz and Sosnick, *Budget's New Clothes*, pp. 78-86.

40. Ibid., pp. 110-22.

41. Ibid., pp. 146, 155.

42. Ibid., pp. 268-71.

43. Ibid.

44. Wildavsky, "Rescuing Policy Analysis from PPBS," p. 463.

45. Ibid., pp. 461, 462.

46. Dror, *Public Policymaking Re-Examined*, p. 81.

47. See Chapter 1.

48. See the previous section.

49. Ibid.

50. For a more detailed explanation of these models, read Charles E. Lindblom, "The Science of Muddling Through," *Public Administration Review* 19, no. 2 (Spring 1959); with David Braybrooke, *A Strategy of Decision* (New York: Free Press of Glencoe, 1963); Aaron Wildavsky, *The Politics of the Budgetary Process* (Boston: Little Brown, 1964).

51. Wildavsky, "Rescuing Policy Analysis from PPBS," pp. 462-63.

52. Dror, *Public Policymaking Re-Examined*, p. 133.

53. Wildavsky, "Rescuing Policy Analysis from PPBS," pp. 463, 474.

54. Author's conclusion.

55. Frederick C. Mosher, "New Integrated Systems for Planning, Programming, and Budgeting" (paper prepared for the XVth International Congress of Administrative Science, 1971), p. 1.

56. Interview, Robert Wallace (OMB Deputy Director Malick's special assistant) on 11 October 1973.

57. Wildavsky, "Rescuing Policy Analysis from PPBS," pp. 461, 462.

58. Thomas J. Cook and Frank P. Scioli, Jr., "Resources for Public Policy Analysis," *Policy Studies Journal* 1, no. 2 (Winter 1970), p. 61.

59. Wildavsky, "Rescuing Policy Analysis from PPBS," pp. 462-65.

Bibliography

Bibliography

Books

Alfandary-Alexander, Mand, ed. *Analysis for Planning, Programming and Budgeting: Proceeding of the Second Cost-Effectiveness Symposium.* Washington, D.C.: Washington Operations Research Council, 1968.

Bauer, Raymond A., and Gergen, Kenneth J. *The Study of Policy Formation.* New York: The Free Press, 1968.

Black, Guy. *The Application of Systems Analysis to Government Operations.* New York: Frederick A. Praeger, 1968.

Burkhead, Jesse. *Government Budgeting.* New York: John Wiley and Sons, Inc., 1956, 1965.

Chartrand, Robert T.; Janda, Kenneth; and Hugo, Michael, eds. *Information Support, Program Budgeting and the Congress.* New York: Spartan Books, 1968.

Committee for Economic Development. *Improving Executive Management in the Federal Government.* New York: Committee for Economic Development, 1964.

Davis, James W., Jr., ed. *Politics, Programs, and Budgets.* Englewood Cliffs, N.J.: Prentice-Hall, Inc., 1969.

Doh, Joon Chien. *The Planning-Programming-Budgeting System in Three Federal Agencies.* Washington, D.C.: Praeger Publishers, 1971.

Dror, Yehezkel. *Public Policymaking Re-Examined.* San Francisco: Chandler Publishing Company, 1968.

Dye, Thomas R. *Understanding Public Policy.* Englewood Cliffs, N.J.: Prentice-Hall, 1972.

Easton, David. *The Political System.* New York: Alfred A. Knopf, 1953.

Galbraith, John K. *The Affluent Society.* 2nd ed. Boston, Mass.: Houghton Mifflin Co., 1962.

Harrington, Michael. *The Other America.* Baltimore, Md.: Penguin Books, Inc., 1962.

Hartley, Harry J. *Educational Planning-Programming-Budgeting: A Systems Approach.* Englewood Cliffs, N.J.: Prentice-Hall, 1968.

Hatry, Harry P., and Cotton, John F. *Program Planning for State, County and City.* Washington, D.C.: State-Local Finance Project of the George Washington University, 1967.

Haveman, Robert, and Margolis, Julius, eds. *Public Expenditures and Policy Analysis.* Chicago: Markham Publishing Co., 1970.

Hinrichs, Harley H., and Taylor, Graeme M. *Program Budgeting and Benefit-Cost Analysis.* Pacific Palisades, Calif.: Goodyear, 1969.

Hitch, Charles J., and McKean, Roland N. *The Economics of Defense in the Nuclear Age.* New York: Atheneum, 1970.

121

Hoos, Ida R. *Systems Analysis in Public Policy.* Berkeley, Calif.: University of California Press, 1972.

Hovey, Harold A. *The Planning-Programming-Budgeting Approach to Government Decision Making.* New York: Frederick A. Praeger, 1968.

Lasswell, Harold D. *Politics: Who Gets What, When, How.* New York: McGraw-Hill Book Co., 1936.

Lindblom, Charles E. *The Intelligence of Democracy.* Glencoe, N.Y.: The Free Press, 1965.

_____. *The Policy-Making Process.* Englewood Cliffs, N.J.: Prentice-Hall, Inc., 1968.

_____, and Braybrooke, David. *A Strategy of Decision.* New York: Free Press of Glencoe, 1963.

Lyden, Fremont J., and Miller, Ernest G., eds. *Planning, Programming Budgeting: A Systems Approach to Management.* Chicago: Markham Publishing Co., 1967, 1972.

March, James G., and Simon, Herbert A. *Organization.* New York: John Wiley, 1958.

Merewitz, Leonard, and Sosnick, Stephen H. *The Budget's New Clothes.* Chicago: Markham Publishing Co., 1971.

National Bureau of Economic Research. *The Rate and Direction of Inventive Activity.* Princeton, N.J.: Princeton University Press, 1962.

New York Bureau of Municipal Research. *Making a Municipal Budget.* New York: Bureau of Municipal Research, 1907.

New York State. Division of the Budget. *Guidelines for Integrated Planning, Programming, Budgeting, 1967.* Albany, N.Y.

Novick, David. *Efficiency and Economy in Government Through New Budgeting and Accounting Procedures.* Santa Monica, Calif.: The Rand Corporation, 1954. R-254.

_____. *A New Approach to the Military Budget.* Santa Monica, Calif.: The Rand Corporation, 1956. RM-1759.

_____, ed. *Program Budgeting.* Cambridge, Mass.: Harvard University Press, 1965.

Ott, David J., and Ott, Attiat F. *Federal Budget Policy.* Washington, D.C.: The Brookings Institution, 1965.

Rivlin, Alice M. *Systematic Thinking for Social Action.* Washington, D.C.: The Brookings Institution, 1971.

Rourke, Frances E. *Bureaucracy, Politics and Public Policy.* Boston: Little, Brown and Company, 1969.

Schein, Edgar H. *Process Consultation: Its Role in Organization Development.* Reading, Mass.: Addison-Wesley Publishing Company, 1969.

Schultz, Charles L. *The Politics of Economics and Public Spending.* Washington, D.C.: The Brookings Institution, 1968.

Sharkansky, Ira, ed. *Policy Analysis in Political Science.* Chicago: Markham Publishing Co., 1970.

Simon, Herbert H. *Models of Man.* New York: John Wiley, 1957.

Smithies, Arthur. *The Budgetary Process in the United States.* New York: McGraw-Hill Book Co., Inc., 1955.

Stanley, David T.; Mann, Dean E.; and Doig, Jameson W. *Men Who Govern.* Washington, D.C.: The Brookings Institution, 1967.

Steiss, Alan Walter. *Public Budgeting and Management.* Lexington, Mass.: Lexington Books, 1972.

Truman, David. *The Governmental Process.* New York: Alfred A. Knopf, Inc., 1951.

Wildavsky, Aaron. *The Politics of the Budgetary Process.* Boston: Little, Brown and Company, 1964.

Williams, Walter. *Social Policy Research and Analysis.* New York: American Elsevier Publishing Company, Inc., 1971.

Woll, Peter. *American Bureaucracy.* New York: W.W. Norton and Company, Inc., 1963.

_____, ed. *Public Administration and Policy.* New York: Harper Torchbooks, 1966.

Wright, Chester, and Tate, Michael D., eds. *Economics and System Analysis: Introduction for Public Managers.* Reading, Mass.: Addison-Wesley Publishing Company, 1973.

Articles and Periodicals

American Transit Association. *Bulletin.* July 28, 1971.

Anderson, Jack. "The Washington Merry-Go-Round" *Washington Post*, November 9, 1972.

Anthony, Robert. "Closing the Loop Between Planning and Performance." *Public Administration Review* 31, no. 3 (May/June 1971): 388-98.

Bickner, Robert E. "I Don't Know PPB at All." *Policy Science* 2 (1971): 301-4.

Black, Guy. "Externalities and Structure in PPB." *Public Administration Review* 31, no. 6 (November/December 1971): 637-43.

Botner, Stanley B. "Four Years of PPBS: An Appraisal." *Public Administration Review* 30, no. 4 (July/August 1970): 423-31.

Braestrup, Peter. "$10.6 Billion Housing Bill Is Rejected." *Washington Post*, 28 September 1972.

Burby, John F. "Urban Report/Mass Transit Agency Faces Planning Problems in Shift from Rags to Riches." *National Journal* 2, no. 40 (3 October 1970): 2152-59.

Capron, William M. "PPB and State Budgeting." *Public Administration Review* 29, no. 2 (March/April 1969): 155-59.

Churchman, C.W., and Schainblatt, A.H. "PPB: How Can It Be Implemented?" *Public Administration Review* 29, no. 2 (March/April 1969): 178-88.

Cohn, Victor. "U.S. Seeks New Ways to Improve Transport." *Washington Post*, 3 February 1972.

Cook, Thomas J., and Scioli, Frank, Jr. "Resources for Public Policy Analysis." *Policy Studies Journal* 1, no. 2 (Winter 1972), 61-63.

"Dozen Cities Planning or Building Transit Lines." *New York Times*, 29 January 1972.

Dror, Yehezkel. "PPB and the Public Policy-Making System: Some Reflections on the Papers by Bertram M. Goss and Allen Schick." *Public Administration Review* 29, no. 2 (March/April 1969): 152-54.

Eisen, Jack. "Transit Leaders Plead for Subsidy at Senate Hearing." *Washington Post*, 1 February 1972.

"End of the Line." *Wall Street Journal*, 7 August 1970.

Fenno, Richard F. "The Impact of PPBS on the Congressional Appropriation Process." *Information Support, Program Budgeting and the Congress.* Edited by Robert T. Chartrand, Kenneth Janda, and Michael Hugo. New York: Spartan Books, 1968.

Fletcher, Stephen M. "From PPBS to PAR in the Empire State." *State Government* (Council of State Governments, Lexington, Ky.) 45 (Summer 1972): 190-202.

Gross, Bertram M. "The New Systems Budgeting." *Public Administration Review* 29, no. 2 (March/April 1969): 113-36.

Harper, Edwin L.; Kramer, Fred A.; and Rouse, Andrew M. "The Implementation and Use of PPB in Sixteen Federal Agencies." *Public Administration Review* 29, no. 6 (November/December 1969): 623-32.

Hatry, Harry. "Status of PPBS in Local and State Governments in the United States." *Policy Science* 2 (1971): 177-89.

Herbert, Ray. "Air Cushion Train Plan Hits Board Roadblock." *Los Angeles Times*, 5 November 1971.

Hirsch, Werner Z. "Toward Federal Program Budgeting." *Public Administration Review* 26, no. 4 (December 1966): 259-70.

Howard, S. Kenneth. "The PPB Game." *Public Administration Review* 30, no. 2 (March/April): 193-94.

Institute of Rail Transit. *Digest*, no. 8 (January-February 1972) and no. 9 (March-April 1972).

Karr, Albert R. "Transit Boosters Complain that Administration Is Holding Back Funds Already Okayed by Congress." *Wall Street Journal*, 24 December 1971.

Klein, Burton H. "The Decision-Making Problem in Development." National Bureau of Economic Research. *The Rate and Direction of Inventive Activity.* Princeton, N.J.: Princeton University Press, 1962.

Lilley, William III. "Urban Report/Transit Lobby Sights Victory in Fight for Massive Subsidy Program." *National Journal* 40 (March 4, 1972): 393-403.

_____. "Urban Report/Urban Interests Win Transit Bill with 'Letter Perfect' Lobbying." *National Journal* 40 (9 September 1970): 2021-29.

Lindblom, Charles E. "The Science of 'Muddling Through'." *Public Administration Review* 19, no. 2 (Spring 1959): 79-88.

Lindsey, Robert. "U.S. Is Considering Mass Transit Aid." *New York Times*, 2 February 1972.

Lyden, Fremont James. "PPB in Britain." *Public Administration Review* 30, no. 4 (July/August 1970): 435-36.

Miller, Ernest G. "Implementing PPBS: Problems and Prospects." *Public Administration Review* 28, no. 5 (September/October 1968): 466-67.

Millward, Robert E. "PPBS: Problems of Implementation." *AIP Journal* 24, no. 1 (March 1968): 88-93.

Morse, Ellsworth H., Jr. "The Planning-Programming-Budgeting System and the Congress." *Federal Accountant* 2, no. 4 (September 1969): 22-36.

Mosher, Frederick C. "Limitations and Problems of PPBS in the States." *Public Administration Review* 29, no. 2 (March/April 1969): 160-66.

Mushkin, Selma J. "PPB in Cities." *Public Administration Review* 29, no. 2 (March/April 1969), 167-77.

Passenger Transport. 4 and 25 February, 3 March, 2 and 16 June, 1972.

Quade, E.S. "Systems Analysis Techniques for Planning-Programming-Budgeting." *Planning-Programming-Budgeting.* Edited by Fremont J. Lyden and Ernest G. Miller. 2nd ed. Chicago: Markham Publishing Co., 1972.

Reuss, Henry S. "A Breakthrough in New Urban Transport Systems." *Traffic Quarterly* 20, no. 1 (January 1966): 21-30.

_____ . "Research Is Needed to Develop New Modes of Urban Transport." *Transportation Journal* 5, no. 4 (Winter 1965): 21-26.

Schick, Allen. "A Death in the Bureaucracy: The Demise of Federal PPB." *Public Administration Review* 33, no. 2 (March/April 1973): 146-56.

_____ . "PPB: The View from the States." *State Government* (Council of State Governments, Lexington, Ky.) 45, no. 4 (Winter 1972): 12-19.

_____ . "The Road to PPB: The Stages of Budget Reform." *Public Administration Review* 26, no. 4 (December 1966): 243-58.

_____ . "Systems Politics and Systems Budgeting." *Public Administration Review* 29, no. 2 (March/April 1969): 137-51.

"Transit Leaders Plead for Subsidy at Senate Hearing." *Washington Post*, 1 February 1972.

"Transit Subsidy Approved." *Washington Post*, 17 February 1972.

White, Michael J. "The Impact of Management Science on Political Decision Making." *Planning-Programming-Budgeting.* Edited by Fremont J. Lyden and Ernest G. Miller. 2nd ed. Chicago: Markham Publishing Co., 1972.

Wildavsky, Aaron. "The Political Economy of Efficiency: Cost-Benefit Analysis, System Analysis and Program Budgeting." *Public Administration Review* 26, no. 4 (December 1966): 292-310.

_____ . "Rescuing Policy Analysis from PPBS." *Public Administration Review* 29, no. 2 (March/April 1969): 189-202.

U.S. Government Publications

The Comptroller General of the United States. *Survey of Progress in Implementing the Planning-Programming-Budgeting System in Executive Agencies.* Report to the Congress, 29 July 1969.

U.S. Congress. *Congressional Record*, 1 February 1972, and 2 March 1972.

_____. House. Committee on Appropriations. *Reprogramming for the Dulles TACV Demonstration Project. Hearings* before the Sub-Committee on Transportation. 92d Cong., 1st sess., 23 March 1971.

_____. Committee on Government Operations. *The Budget Process in the Federal Government.* Washington, D.C.: U.S. Government Printing Office, 1969.

_____. Joint Economic Committee. *The Analysis and Evaluation of Public Expenditures: The PPB System, A Compendium of Papers Submitted to the Sub-Committee on Economy in Government.* 3 vols. Washington, D.C.: U.S. Government Printing Office, 1969.

_____. *Economic Analysis and the Efficiency of Government.* Report of the Sub-Commmittee on Economy in Government. Washington, D.C.: U.S. Government Printing Office, 1970.

_____. *Guidelines for Estimating the Benefits of Public Expenditures. Hearings* before the Sub-Committee on Economy in Government. Washington, D.C.: U.S. Government Printing Office, 1969.

_____. *The Planning-Programming-Budgeting System: Progress and Potential. Hearings* before the Sub-Committee on Economy in Government. Washington, D.C.: U.S. Government Printing Office, 1967.

_____. Senate. Committee on Banking and Currency. *Report* to Accompany S.3700 together with individual views (Urban Mass Transportation Amendments of 1966), 8 August 1966. Washington, D.C.: U.S. Government Printing Office, 1966.

_____. Committee on Government Operations. *Planning-Programming-Budgeting. Hearings* before the Sub-Committee on National Security and International Affairs. 90th Cong., 1st sess., 23 August 1967.

_____. "Program Budgeting in Foreign Affairs: Some Reflections," by Frederick C. Mosher. Prepared for the Sub-Committee on National Security and International Organizations. Washington, D.C.: U.S. Government Printing Office, 1970.

_____. Senate. Committee on Government Operations. *Planning, Programming, Budgeting.* Inquiry of the Sub-Committee on National Security and International Operations. Washington, D.C.: U.S. Government Printing Office, 1970.

_____. Sub-Committee on National Security and International Operations. *Planning-Programming-Budgeting, Initial Memorandum.* 1967.

U.S. Department of Transportation. Coast Guard. *FY 1973 Spring Preview*, 22 June 1971.

_____. Coast Guard. "FY 1974 Plan Summary for Short-Range Aids to Navigation," n.d.

_____. Coast Guard. *Planning and Programming Manual–1971.* January 1971.

_____. Coast Guard. "Status of Systems Study of Short Range Aids to Navigation," unpublished paper, 1 June 1972.

_____. "DOT Planning-Programming-Budgeting System," DOT *Order* 2400.2A, dated 1/15/69.

_____. "Feasibility of Federal Assistance to Urban Mass Transportation Operating Costs," 22 November 1971.

_____. "FY 1973 Planning and Budgeting Process," DOT *Notice* 5100.1, dated 6/29/71.

_____. *National Plan for Navigation.* May 1970.

_____. *National Plan for Navigation.* April 1972.

_____. Urban Mass Transportation Administration. "Preliminary Report on Criteria and Objectives for UMTA: Programs: A Special Analytical Study for the Bureau of the Budget." June 1970.

_____. Urban Mass Transportation Administration. *Spring Preview of FY 1973.* (Unpublished.)

_____. Urban Mass Transportation Administration. *Spring Preview of FY 1974.* (Unpublished.)

_____. Urban Mass Transportation Administration. "UMTA Planning-Programming-Budgeting System," UMTA *Order* 2400.1.

U.S. Executive Office of the President. Office of Management and Budget. *Bulletin* No. 68-9. April 12, 1968.

_____.Office of Management and Budget. *U.S. Budget, FY 1969.* "Comparison of Old and New Budget Concepts, Special Analysis A." Washington, D.C.: U.S. Government Printing Office.

_____. *U.S. Budget, FY 1969.* "Investments, Operating and Other Budget Outlays, Special Analysis D." Washington, D.C.: U.S. Government Printing Office.

_____. White House Press Release, 12 March 1970.

U.S. National Technical Information Service. *The Politics of Innovation in Urban Mass Transportation Policy Making: The New System Example.* By David G. Lawrence. Washington, D.C.: National Technical Information Service PB 194 098, August 1970.

Urban Mass Transporation Act of 1964, as revised, 78 STAT. 302, 49 U.S.C. 1601 et seq.

Unpublished Materials

Axelrod, Donald. "Planning and Budgeting in the 70's: Responsibility or Social Bankruptcy." Presentation at annual conference of National American Society for Public Administration, Los Angeles, Calif., 3-7 April 1973.

Beggs, James. "Criteria and Objectives for UMTA Programs." Memorandum to Donald B. Rice, 17 February 1971.

_____ . "Criteria and Objectives for the UMTA Programs." Memorandum to Donald B. Rice, 30 April 1971.

Broyhill, Joel, Representative. Letter to Secretary John Volpe, 8 March 1971.

Caputo, David. "Normative and Empirical Implications of Budgetary Processes." Paper prepared for delivery at the annual meeting of the American Political Science Association, Los Angeles, Calif., 8-12 September 1970.

Chief, Office of Marine Environment and Systems, United States Coast Guard. "Format and Content of Plan Summary for Short Range A/N." Memorandum to the Division of Plans Evaluation, August 1971.

Chief of Staff, United States Coast Guard. "Plans for Major Projects for Short-Range Aids to Navigation." Memorandum to the Chief, Office of Operations, 19 July 1971.

Commandant, United States Coast Guard. "FY 1974 Program Determinations." Memorandum to Program Managers, 10 January 1972.

_____ . "FY 1974 Program Guidance." Memorandum, 13 July 1972.

Haley, George, Chief Counsel to UMTA. "Senate Urban Mass Transportation Amendments." Memorandum to C.C. Villarreal, 3 March 1972.

Jackson, Henry M., Senator. Letter to Secretary John Volpe, 2 July 1971.

Korb, Lawrence J. "Budget Strategies of the Joint Chiefs of Staff, (Fiscal) 1965-1968: An Examination." Speech delivered at the annual meeting of the American Political Science Association, Los Angeles, Calif., 8-12 September 1970.

Lynch, Thomas D. "Federal Capital Assistance for Transit Systems." Memorandum to Milton L. Brooks, 30 September 1971.

McKinsey and Co., Inc. *Strengthening Planning, Programming and Budgeting in the Bureau of the Budget.* June 1969. (Unpublished.)

McManus, Robert. "Discussion Paper, Alternative Operating Grant Program." Memorandum to C.C. Villarreal, 24 January 1972.

_____ . "Implementing Revised Criteria and Objectives for UMTA Capital Grant Program." Draft memorandum from C.C. Villarreal to John Ollson, 17 April 1971.

_____ . "Revision of the UMTA Capital Grant Criteria." Memorandum to Fred Meister (OMB), 14 March 1972.

_____ . "Revision of the UMTA Capital Grant Criteria." Memorandum to William Hurd, 14 March 1972.

_____ . "Status of the New Criteria and/or Evaluation of Capital Grant Criteria." Memorandum to William Allison, 5 October 1971.

_____ . "Testimony on Federal Mass Transit Operating Subsidies." Memorandum to Barclay Webber, DOT General Counsel in charge of legislative testimony, 5 June 1972.

_____ . "UMTA Capital Grant Objectives and Criteria." Memorandum from C.C. Villarreal to James Beggs, 24 April 1972.

Mayo, Robert P. Letter to Secretary John Volpe, 2 February 1970.

Mosher, Frederick C. "New Integrated Systems for Planning, Programming, Budgeting." Paper prepared for the XVth International Congress of Administrative Science, 1971.

Murray, Gordon. Letter to William R. MacDougall, 29 June 1971.

_____ . "Meeting on Capital Grant Criteria." Note to C.C. Villarreal, 12 July 1971.

Muth, H.D., Acting Chief, Office of Marine Environment and Systems. "FY 1974 Budget Planning Cycle." Memorandum to Aids to Navigation Division, 17 August 1971.

Niskanen, William A. Presentation at Second Annual National Capital Area Chapter, American Society for Public Administration, panel titled "Program Budgeting and Analysis—What's New?" Washington, D.C., 30 September 1971.

_____ . "Why New Methods of Budgetary Choice?" Paper delivered at the International Institute of Public Finance, Nuremberg, Germany, September 1971.

Prestemon, Robert. "Program Issues for the FY 1974 Program Planning and Budgeting Process (Spring Preview)." Memorandum to UMTA, 21 March 1972.

Rice, Donald B., Assistant Director of OMB. "OMB Recommendations Concerning Criteria and Objectives for UMTA Programs." Memorandum to Undersecretary James Beggs, 9 February 1971.

Spong, William B., Jr., Senator. Letter to Secretary John Volpe, 2 April 1972.

Villarreal, C.C., UMTA Administrator. Memorandum re Draft Study. Memorandum to key UMTA, DOT and OMB staff, 12 November 1970.

_____ . "OMB Recommendations Concerning Criteria and Objectives for UMTA Programs." Memorandum to James Beggs, 16 February 1971.

_____ . "Report on Alternative Assistance Programs." Memorandum to Deputy Under-Secretary and Others, 11 February 1972.

_____ . "Task Force Re: Transit Assistance Grants." Memorandum to Deputy Under-Secretary and Others, 17 December 1971.

_____ . Transmission of final draft of "Criteria and Objectives for the UMTA Program." Memorandum to John Ollson, 17 December 1970.

_____ . "UMTA Capital Grant Objectives and Criteria." Memorandum drafted by Robert McManus to James Beggs, 24 April 1972.

_____ . "UMTA Capital Grant Objectives and Criteria." Memorandum to James Beggs, n.d.

Volpe, John, Secretary. "Implementing Revised Criteria and Objectives for UMTA Capital Grant Programs." Draft memorandum written by Robert McManus, 17 April 1971.

_____ . Letter to Senator Henry M. Jackson, 5 August 1971.

_____ . "Mass Transit Operating Assistance." Memorandum to Presidential Assistant John Ehrlichman and OMB Director George P. Shultz, 7 April 1972.

Interviews

The names of most interviewees are held confidential. Complete documentation of interviews is being held by Professor Lewis Welch, State University of New York at Albany.

About the Author

Thomas D. Lynch is Assistant Director of the Department of Public Administration and an Assistant Professor at the Maxwell School of Citizenship and Public Affairs at Syracuse University. Prior to joining the faculty at Maxwell, Dr. Lynch served as a program analyst with a variety of federal agencies, including the Urban Mass Transportation Administration and the Maritime Administration. He has also been an American Society for Public Administration Fellow in the Department of Housing and Urban Development. Dr. Lynch is editor-in-chief of *The Bureaucrat* and editor of the Occasional Papers Service. Active in the American Society for Public Administration for several years, he serves on that organization's national council.